F

Sigmund Freud

Brief Lives:
Sigmund Freud

David Carter

Brief Lives
Published by Hesperus Press Limited
19 Bulstrode Street, London W1U 2JN
www.hesperuspress.com

First published by Hesperus Press Limited, 2011

Designed and typeset by Fraser Muggeridge studio
Printed in Jordan by Jordan National Press

ISBN: 978-1-84391-922-3

Contents

Introduction

The family history of the man who stressed the importance of family history for an understanding of psychological development must be of particular interest to those seeking insight into his life. However, Sigmund Freud was always guarded and discreet about all matters relating to his family. In many cases it is only possible to state what seems most likely to be true; in some cases one must describe the various possible accounts; and occasionally it is wise to claim only that something is plausible but unverified. Fortunately, however, there are a considerable number of facts on which all biographers agree. Certain, for example, is that he was born at half past six on 6 May 1856, at 117 Schlossergasse in the small Moravian town of Freiberg, now known as Příbor. There have been some attempts to question this date in favour of an earlier one, due to an illegible entry in a birth register, but the evidence for its correctness is not now generally disputed. Biographers have taken pains to stress the uncertainties that accompanied him from birth: had his father had two or three wives, and how could he already be the uncle of a boy older than himself?

There is also little documentary evidence for the origins of the Freud family. Freud's own account in his short autobiographical essay of 1925 is based on family hearsay. It seems that his father met the secretary of the Jewish community in Cologne one day by chance, and the man told him that the Freuds could trace their descent back to that city in the fourteenth century. Freud claimed that his ancestors were among those Jews who fled persecution by moving eastward in the fourteenth and fifteenth centuries. In the course of the nineteenth century they moved further, from Lithuania into Galicia. Here the family divided, one part to Romania and the other to Moravia.

The main sources for Freud's life consist of his own voluminous correspondence, his 'Autobiographical Study' of 1925, personal reflections and allusions in his psychoanalytic writings, and the major biographies. Among these, that by Ernest Jones, due to his personal contacts with Freud and his family, and despite its weaknesses and biases, remains indispensable. Peter Gay's *Freud, A Life for Our Time*, demands respect for its thorough evaluation of evidence. It contains also an impressive 'Bibliographical Essay', but an idiosyncratic system of annotations. It blends well accounts of the life, the works and the cultural and historical background.

The present biographer has the advantages and limits of a 'Brief Life'. It must of necessity focus on the events involving Freud and his family, with consideration of other persons only as they impinge on that life. The advantage of a short biography, following a strict chronological sequence, is that it can bring into relief the overall development of the life. In the major bio graphies, as excellent as they are, it is often difficult to see the wood for the trees.

A problem for all biographers is how to divide up the constant flow of a life into chapters. I have opted to highlight major features of the periods in the chapter headings.

I would also like to express my very belated appreciation of the help provided by Anna Freud and the family maid Paula Fichtl, while researching for my Ph.D. on Freud in what was then still the Freud family home in Maresfield Gardens, London.

Childhood and Adolescence
(1856–73)

Freud's biographer Ernest Jones has stated unequivocally that Freud's father, Jakob, had two wives, but Peter Gay has stated just as unequivocally that he had three. Whatever the truth of the matter, Sigmund was the son of the last of them, born Amalie Nathansohn (the most commonly accepted spellings for both names). Jakob was a wool merchant, though not very well off. His mother came from the north-eastern part of Galicia near the Russian frontier. They were married in 1855, when Jakob was already forty. She was only twenty-one when she had her first child, whose name was registered in the family Bible as 'Sigismund Schlomo', the latter after his paternal grandfather. By the time he entered the University of Vienna in 1873, Freud had developed a firm preference for the form 'Sigmund'. When Jakob married Amalie in 1855, he had two sons from his first marriage: Emanuel, already married with children; and the younger one, Philipp, unmarried. Emanuel's son, John, was a year older than his uncle Sigismund Schlomo, who for the sake of simplicity will be henceforth referred to only as Sigmund. Sigmund and John became firm friends and Freud later admitted that this relationship had conditioned the way he was to conduct many of his friendships in later life.

Amalie was to bear seven more children: Julius, who only survived for eight months; Anna, in December 1858, when Sigmund was in his third year; Rosa; Marie (known as Mitzi); Adolfine (known as Dolfi); Paula; and Alexander. In later correspondence Freud was to admit that the death of young Julius had undoubtedly affected him deeply. He believed that the advent of the young child, depriving him of his mother's full attention, had awoken death wishes against his young brother, and when the child eventually died he developed a sense of guilt for having had such thoughts that was to stay with him for a long time.

Most influential on his psychological development seems to have been not his relationship with his siblings but that with his nephew John. His feelings for John were alternately affectionate and hostile. Freud commented in later years that this combination of contrasting feelings was to have a determining effect on how he developed all of his later friendships with people of the same age. He felt that an intimate friend and a hated enemy had always been indispensable to his emotional life, and sometimes they had coincided in the same person, albeit not at the same time as in his childhood relationship with John. Freud was later to recall an adventure he shared with John when he was about three years old, and involving John's sister Pauline. In this memory Sigmund and John had been collecting flowers in a meadow in the company of Pauline. They suddenly turned on the girl, attacking her physically, and possibly sexually, taking away her bunch of flowers.

Another person who featured prominently in Freud's early life and later in his self-analysis was his nanny, a devout Roman Catholic, who was apparently old and ugly and often dragged young Sigmund off to church with her. He seems to have loved her though, and may even have learned about sexual matters from her (another one of those plausible but unverified facts). Round about the time when his mother was giving birth to his sister Anna, the nanny suddenly disappeared. Freud later discovered that she had been caught stealing and that his half-brother Philipp had insisted on her being arrested. The upshot was that she was sent to prison for ten months. Freud retained an odd memory of this incident, in which he clearly associated his mother's 'absence' with the disappearance of the nanny. The significance of the memory he only unravelled in the course of his self-analysis about forty years later. In the memory he saw himself standing in front of a chest, which Philipp was holding half-open. The young Sigmund, in tears, was asking him something. Finally, his mother, looking slim and not pregnant, came into the room. Freud recalled also that when the nanny had disappeared, he had suspected Philipp of somehow being the cause of this and had asked his half-brother what had happened to her. Philipp had replied 'Sie ist eingekastelt.' This means literally 'She has been put in a chest,' but it was a current idiom meaning 'She has been put in prison.' Freud could thus construe his memory as a child's literal interpretation of Philipp's words. As Philipp and his mother were of a similar age, Freud believed that the memory indicated a childish fear that Philipp might also be responsible for his mother's 'absence'; in other words, that Philipp was the father of the new baby. Remembering the opening of an empty chest and the appearance of a slim mother were thus ways of reassuring himself that this was not the case.

Some writers have accused Freud of being excessively concerned with financial matters. Money did concern him, but no more than his circumstances merited, as will be explained in due course. Undoubtedly the economic hardship of his parents during his childhood made him conscious of the need to acquire a measure of financial security. When Freud was born, his parents were living in one rented room in a small house owned by the local blacksmith. His father had seen better days, but in the previous twenty years there had been a steady decline in the textile trade. With Czech nationalism on the rise there was much antipathy towards the German-speaking Austrians and the Jews. Even in the small town of Freiberg the Jewish merchants were seen to be the cause of the decline in the textile industry. Gradually Jakob Freud came to realise that there was no future for him and his family in the area, and in 1859, when Sigmund was three years old, they moved to Leipzig. But, finding few business opportunities there, they moved one year later to Vienna.

The Freuds' first home in Vienna was in the Pfeffergasse in the mainly Jewish quarter of Leopoldstadt, not far from the famous recreational area known as the Prater. At the age of nine, in 1865, Sigmund passed the entrance examination one year earlier than was usual, enabling him to attend secondary school. The one he attended was known as the 'Leopoldstädter Kommunalreal- und Obergymnasium'. After it expanded into the Sperlgasse in 1870 it was known as the 'Sperlgymnasium'. Here he was an exceptionally good student, coming top of his class for the last six of his eight years there (Freud would later remember this to be the last seven years). In 1865, however, the family was to suffer the disgrace of having one of its members accused of criminal activity. Jakob's brother Joseph was eventually found guilty of and imprisoned for dealing in counterfeit roubles.

Freud had various interesting memories of events in his childhood which are difficult to date precisely. One, which he believed happened when he was ten or twelve years old, concerned his father, who often used to take his son with him on walks. During such walks his father would talk about his experiences and past events. On one occasion his father wanted to impress upon him how much the situation of the Jews in Austria had improved since he was young. He told of a Saturday evening in Freiberg when he was taking a walk with a new fur cap on, with which he was obviously very pleased. Suddenly a passing Christian knocked his brand new cap off and told him in no uncertain terms what he thought of Jews getting in his way. Obviously expecting that his father would have made some protest, Sigmund asked him how he responded, to which his father replied that he just stepped into the road and picked up his cap. Freud was clearly ashamed and hurt by his father's demeaning behaviour and never forgot it. As though in compensation for his disappointment, he cultivated an interest in famous heroic individuals such as Hannibal and Alexander the Great.

It should also be noted that from childhood Freud was a voracious reader. He admitted that he had been greatly influenced by his early reading of the Bible, but it is likely to have been the dramatic events and moral tales that impressed him more than the specifically Christian message. By his own admission it seems that he did not read his first modern novel until he was about thirteen, though he knew already many works by classic German authors. In a letter to his future wife Martha Bernays on 14 January 1884, he claimed to have started reading Shakespeare at the age of eight, though how much he read in the original English is unclear. He was, however, developing some facility in several languages: Latin, Greek and Hebrew, English and French, and had taught himself some Italian and Spanish. Ernest Jones claims that Freud had once told him he was especially fond of English and that at one period of his life he had spent ten years reading nothing but English books.[1]

In 1872, when he was sixteen, there occurred Freud's first recorded experience of love. Details of this are to be found in the correspondence between Freud and his bosom friend of those years, Eduard Silberstein. Silberstein had stayed in Freiberg, but they maintained their friendship through frequent letters. While at school together in Freiberg they had learned Spanish and developed their own private mythology and language, speaking and writing in a mixture of German and Spanish. They formed their own secret society which was called the *Academia Cartellana*, and they addressed each other by the names of two dogs in a philosophical dialogue by Cervantes: Freud was Cipion and Silberstein was Berganza. It was on a return visit to Freiberg to see Silberstein, other old friends and the countryside he loved that Freud was smitten.

During his visit to Freiberg Sigmund stayed with the Fluss family who were old friends of his parents, the fathers being in the same business of textiles. He had known their daughter, Gisela, when they were both small children, but now, with her just a year or so younger than him, he was bowled over by her charms. He did not have the chance to communicate his feelings to her, due partly to his own shyness but also because she went off to school only a few days after his arrival. On his return to Vienna, however, Sigmund poured his heart out in his letters to Silberstein. It remained very much a one-sided love and nothing ever came of it. Yet a close study of the correspondence with Silberstein reveals some interesting aspects of the whole affair, providing insight into his preferences in matters of the heart which the older Freud might have described as Oedipal in origin. While writing ostensibly about Gisela, Freud praised at great length the charms, intelligence and sensitivity of Gisela's mother, Frau Fluss. From the letters it is clear that he was quite aware of what he was doing: transferring respect and affection for the mother to the daughter.

The obsession with Gisela did not last long because Freud soon had to turn his attention to deciding what he was going to study at university. In 1773, at the age of seventeen, he graduated from the Sperlgymnasium with the highest distinction possible. The results of the final examinations confirm his linguistic abilities. Noteworthy and of some relevance to the development of his ideas is the fact that in the Greek exam he had to translate twenty-three verses of Sophocles' *Oedipus* from Greek into German. His father's reward was to promise him a trip to England, which was eventually to be realised when he was nineteen. (Sigmund's half-brother Emanuel, together with his wife and two children, and his brother Philipp had already moved to Manchester.)

Sigmund took some time considering the field of study he would enter at university. At first, it seems, under the influence of his friendship with an older boy at the Sperlgymnasium, a certain Heinrich Braun, who would later become a prominent Social Democratic politician in Austria, he considered studying law and involving himself in social issues. But something in him was seeking an understanding of the world at a deeper level than politics, and he recalled later that the ideas of Darwin, then becoming widely known, were starting to have a powerful influence on him. One experience seems to have tipped the balance in favour of natural science, though it could have only been the culmination of a long-gestating process. Freud attended a popular lecture by the professor of zootomy and comparative anatomist Carl Brühl, who was apparently a powerful and compelling speaker. Brühl included in his lecture a reading of an essay which was then considered to be by Goethe but has since been identified as the work of the Swiss writer Christoph Tobler, an acquaintance of Goethe. The essay is essentially a prose hymn of praise to Mother Nature, written in very emotive tones. It could hardly have persuaded Freud in any logical sense, but perhaps it gave him the confidence of his conviction that the study of nature was his true calling. For several months in early 1873 he wrote teasing letters to his old friend Emil Fluss, the brother of that very Gisela, indicating that he had come to a momentous decision about his future. Finally he wrote to him on 1 May revealing his decision to become a natural scientist.

What Freud understood by natural science and hoped to gain from the study of nature was clearly not, however, mere dry academic knowledge. The field of natural science he finally opted for was medicine, but in his 'Autobiographical Study' of 1925 he stressed that he had felt no special desire to become a medical practitioner at that time and had been obsessed rather by a powerful desire for knowledge. In his correspondence to friends such as Fluss, even before he made known his firm decision of 1873, he stressed that this powerful desire for knowledge was focused not so much on the natural world as on human nature.

The Student Years: Cocaine and Courtship (1873–85)

Much has been made of the effect of anti-Semitism on Freud's career, and he emphasised it in his 'Autobiographical Study'. As a student at the University of Vienna it was frequently made clear to him by gentile students he encountered that he was not truly Austrian and that he should recognise his inferiority to them. His response was a firm refusal to accept such a status as second-class citizen. If anything he seems to have drawn some satisfaction from the feeling of being different. Being an outsider only strengthened him in his belief in the need for independence of judgement.

From the start Sigmund was determined not to follow blindly the prescribed courses for medical students but to take the opportunity to broaden his knowledge and interests. He wrote at that time to his friend Silberstein that he planned to spend the first year at university studying many subjects in the field of the humanities, which would probably not be useful to him at all in his future profession. Research has yielded a complete list of the courses he followed, revealing that he nevertheless fulfilled the requirements of his chosen area.[2] In addition he took a course on Darwin's ideas and one by Ernst Brücke, who was to play an influential role in his development later, on the physiology of voice and speech. In the winter semester of 1874 to 1875 he also attended a reading seminar on philosophy with the famous Franz Brentano. In the summer semester of 1875 he added a special course of Brentano's on Aristotle's logic. It is interesting to note too that the philosopher he admired most at this time, according to a letter during that year to Silberstein, was Ludwig Feuerbach. Freud would undoubtedly have been attracted to Feuerbach's critique of theology.

It was in the early summer of 1875 that Freud made his first visit to England, the fulfilment of the promise made to him by his father. He was warmly received by his relatives in Manchester, so much so that he started to wonder, in his correspondence with Silberstein for example, whether it might be a good idea to move to that country. To Silberstein he also confessed his preference for the English mode of scientific thought, citing the empiricism of Huxley, Darwin and others. He was learning to distrust all metaphysics and philosophy in general. Later correspondence with Martha Bernays reveals that the influence England had on Freud was to be long-lasting.

Also in 1875, the Freud family moved to a larger apartment in the Kaiser Josefstrasse, where they stayed until 1885. There were three bedrooms, a living room, dining room and a small study. The family now consisted of eight people, so it was not exactly spacious. As there was no bathroom, a large wooden tub and a supply of hot water was brought into the kitchen once every fortnight to enable the family to take baths. When the children were old enough, they made use of the public baths. The study, a long, narrow room overlooking the street and known as the 'cabinet', was soon allotted to the studious Sigmund. He stayed there throughout the rest of his university life until he became an intern at the hospital. When preoccupied with his studies he would even eat his evening meal there. His sister Anna reported his helping his younger siblings with their studies and advising them on their reading habits from there. His needs were always regarded as paramount in the family; when Sigmund complained that Anna's piano practice was disturbing him, the piano promptly disappeared; an early sign of his lifelong insensitivity to music, apart from that of the greatest and most popular composers.

At the end of the winter semester in March 1876 Freud was able to start some original research. The idea was suggested to him by Professor Carl Claus, head of the Institute of Comparative Anatomy, who had also founded one of the first zoological experimental stations in the world at Trieste on the Adriatic. Freud was one of the first students to be given a grant to conduct research there for several weeks, and he made two visits during the summer term of 1876. The subject of his research may seem obscure but it was a problem which had puzzled philosophers and scientists since Aristotle: why was it impossible to find an adult male eel? No eel had ever been found with mature testes. The theory had long been that the problem was somehow related to the eel's long migration prior to mating. In 1874 a scientist at Trieste had discovered one organ in the eel which he thought might be the missing testes, so Claus sent Freud to check the evidence. Freud's researches provided no firm evidence but did not exclude the possibility. It was useful research and Claus had it published in April 1877, but Freud had obviously been hoping to produce something more ground-breaking, and was generally disappointed with his first experience of research.

During the rest of his studies Freud turned away from anatomy towards physiology, finding a more congenial working environment in Ernst Brücke's laboratory. Brücke, forty years older than Freud, became something of a father figure for him, and from then on he focused specifically on his medical studies. Brücke's philosophy of science was to prove highly influential on Freud's thinking. He belonged very much to the nineteenth century positivist tradition, which attempted to verify all knowledge on a scientific basis. As a medical student in Berlin in the early 1840s Brücke had, together with the highly respected Emil Du Bois-Reymond, rejected all mystical theories that had found their way into scientific thought. For him there was no room for pantheism, superstition, vitalism and the like, and the suppositions of theology had no role in scientific thinking. Together with the great Hermann Helmholtz, who adopted a similar approach in the wide range of fields in which he conducted research (physics, biology, thermodynamics, etc.), he represented the dominant mode of scientific thought at the time when Freud was a student. Through his contact with Brücke, Freud also made a friend who would be very influential in the development of psychoanalysis: the wealthy, eminent physiologist Josef Breuer, who was fourteen years older than him. Freud was soon a regular visitor at Breuer's home, becoming a good friend also to Breuer's wife.

The first project that Freud undertook with Brücke was related to the histology of the nerve cells. The nature of the nervous system in higher animals was a controversial issue at the time, but Freud's research was on some newly discovered cells in the spinal cord of a primitive genus of fish known as the amoecetes (also known as petromyzon). It was published soon after its presentation at the Academy of Sciences in January 1877, and was thus Freud's first published work, pre-dating the publication of the paper for Claus. It had considerable scientific value in helping to close the gap in knowledge about the connections between the nervous systems of lower and of higher animals. Freud's next project, which was started in the summer of 1879, was on the nerve cells of the crayfish. This was also successfully presented at the Academy of Sciences in December 1881, and published in January 1882. These early papers contributed greatly to the later development of the so-called neurone theory.

The two and a half year gap between the start of the crayfish research and its presentation was due partly to the unwelcome obligation of a year's military service from 1879 to 1880. Freud's duties were not arduous; he simply had to look after sick soldiers. Official reports indicate that he carried out his duties with great care and consideration for his patients' needs. He used much of his spare time to translate four essays by John Stuart Mill. Franz Brentano had recommended Freud to the editor of the German edition of Mill's works, Theodor Gomperz. Three of the essays, on socialism, women's franchise and the labour question, were, by Mill's own admission, largely by his wife, but the fourth, on Grote's *Plato*, was entirely by Mill. As Freud later said that his knowledge of Plato was very fragmentary, it seems likely that much of it was gleaned while translating this essay. Mill's favourable analysis of Plato's theory of reminiscence would undoubtedly have intrigued Freud. Partly due to this hiatus in his studies therefore, he did not take his final medical degree until the spring of 1881. After this he stayed on at Brücke's laboratory until the summer of 1882, having been promoted in May 1881 to the post of demonstrator, which carried with it some teaching responsibilities. This appointment lasted till July 1882, when he felt it necessary to take on a junior post at the General Hospital in Vienna for financial reasons. Another important factor in this decision was his meeting with the woman who was to provide him with a family of his own: Martha Bernays.

If Freud had stayed on in Brücke's institute he would undoubtedly have become an assistant, then an assistant professor, and, finally, a professor of physiology. In Freud's autobiographical account it is Brücke who suggests he give up pure research and seek paid employment. But the salary then paid to a university assistant would not have been enough for Freud to support himself and a family. His father, now aged sixty-seven, was in poor financial straits, no longer earning and very dependent on financial help from his wife's family. However, he still had to support seven children. Freud could therefore not expect any substantial help from his family. A strong reason for seeking the appointment in the General Hospital, though it would not bring him much money initially, was that he needed practical experience in the care of patients if he were to make a living as a doctor; university medical courses at that time included no such training. Undoubtedly the most important factor, however, in convincing Freud of the need to seek paid employment in the hospital, was his decision to get married. He had met Martha Bernays, whose family were friends of his family, when she had called on his sister in April 1882. Only two months later, on 17 June, they were engaged.

Martha Bernays came from a distinguished Jewish family. Her father had been secretary to a well-known Viennese economist before dying suddenly of heart failure in 1879. Martha was well-educated but not an intellectual and was quite willing to play the role that Freud envisioned for her. This went even as far as putting her strict orthodox Jewish upbringing behind her to fit in with the views of her husband-to-be. Martha's brother, Eli, became engaged to Freud's sister Anna in June 1882, only six months after his sister's engagement, and they eventually married on 14 October 1883.

The engagement of Sigmund and Martha was to last four and a quarter years, during which time he wrote more than 900 letters to his wife-to-be. After his death his wife expressed the intention several times to burn them, but their daughters persuaded her to preserve them. During the period of their engagement they were separated for three years altogether, and during those periods they wrote daily to each other with only occasional gaps in the correspondence. The reason for the separation was quite simply that she was living with her mother in Wandsbek, near Hamburg, and Freud could not afford to visit her often.

Sigmund's correspondence with Martha is very revealing of his thinking and interests at the time. He wrote to her about virtually everything that was on his mind: his feelings; colleagues; his work; his ambitions; they also frequently discussed literature. Especially interesting is what Sigmund reveals of his expectations of a wife. In this respect he was very much the conventional bourgeois of his day: he believed a wife should look after the welfare and education of the children, supervise household affairs and generally be the sweet, charming creature that nature had intended. He does, however, reveal his belief that the day might well come when relationships between men and women might change under a different education system and women would gain greater rights of individual freedom. Being love letters they also reveal obsessive concern about Martha's health and there are indications of jealousy at any hints of her writing favourably of other men.

Freud's time at the General Hospital was to last about three years. He started as a clinical assistant, and then in May 1883, he became *Sekundärarzt* in the psychiatric clinic of Theodor Meynert. He was subsequently to rise still further: becoming Senior *Sekundärarzt* in July 1884, and in 1885 *Privatdozent*, a post which, while very prestigious, was also unsalaried. During his early days at the hospital he concentrated on surgery. He went on to work in the Division of Internal Medicine under the famous Hermann Nothnagel, who made his students follow a strict regime. While Freud clearly admired him, he started to lose interest in treating the physically sick. Hence it was that he transferred to Meynert's psychiatric clinic in May 1883. It was on this occasion that he moved out of the family home for the first time, at the age of twenty-seven, to live in the hospital. In Meynert's clinic he started to learn more about mental disorders. A form of hallucinatory psychosis had been named 'Meynert's Amentia' after his professor. He worked with Meynert for five months and began to discover how little specialists really understood about the workings of the brain and the nervous system. In October 1883, Freud moved to one of the two departments of dermatology in the hospital. He was particularly interested in exploring the relations between syphilis and diseases of the nervous system. In January 1884, he joined the Department of Nervous Diseases, under the supervision of Franz Scholz.

In the early spring of 1884 Freud started to become interested in the effects of cocaine. At that time little was known about its properties. In a letter to Martha of 21 April he mentioned that there had been reports that a German military doctor had used it successfully to increase the physical endurance of the men in his care, and Freud thought it might be useful in handling cases of nervous exhaustion and possibly in treating the withdrawal symptoms associated with using morphine. He also thought he might be able to use it to wean a friend of his, Ernst von Fleischl-Marxow, off the use of morphine as a painkilling agent. After initial problems in obtaining sufficient quantities, because it was so expensive, Freud experimented with it on himself: one twentieth of a gram changed his bad mood into one of cheerfulness. He noted that it did not deprive him of his ability to work, and it also removed any feelings of hunger; he thought it might therefore have positive effects in preventing vomiting. He also tried it out on Fleischl, who took to it immediately. So enthusiastic did Freud feel that he sent some off to Martha, as a general tonic which would bring colour to her cheeks, and pressed its use on colleagues, friends and members of his family. From a modern perspective he was being somewhat reckless in his recommendations.

Freud completed his first paper on cocaine, 'On Coca', in June 1884, and it was published in a leading medical journal in July. The paper already shows evidence of the easy literary style which was to characterise his later works. It combined a lucid survey of the known history of the plant and its uses, a review of the research already conducted on it, detailed accounts of his own experiments and those of others, and recommendations for its applications. Before going off to see Martha in September he explained the findings of his research to a friend, Leopold Königstein, an ophthalmologist. He had also acquainted another colleague, Carl Koller, with the drug's anaesthetising effects. When he returned to Vienna after seeing Martha, he found that Koller had discovered the usefulness of cocaine as an anaesthetic in certain surgical procedures. Freud was generous in according respect to Koller for his discovery but clearly also disappointed at being away from Vienna at a time when he himself might have won some glory for it. Nevertheless, his paper on cocaine garnered for him a considerable reputation at home and abroad.

Freud was subsequently to be dogged by doubts and a sense of guilt relating to his cocaine researches, due to the fate of his friend Fleischl and to the fact that he had condoned the administration of the drug by injection, though he later denied this. It was a method which other doctors found to have negative side effects. Fleischl's fate was indeed a sad one, and it is easy to understand why Freud, who admitted to Martha that he had deep love and admiration for the man, would want to alleviate his suffering as much as was in his power. At the age of twenty-five, while conducting some anatomical research, Fleischl had become infected in the right hand and had had to have his thumb amputated. The infection stubbornly persisted, however, and he had to undergo several more operations. Fleischl was to remain in a constant state of agony for the rest of his life, which could only be alleviated by morphine. Freud hoped to relieve his friend of his dependence on morphine by the use of cocaine and provided him with his first dose in May 1884. For a while it seemed to work, but then the excruciating pain returned. By the early part of 1885, Freud was spending many nights nursing his friend, who eventually developed chronic cocaine intoxication. Freud expected him to last for only another six months or so, but in fact his agony dragged on for another six years. A companion volume to the present biography contains new translations of all Freud's cocaine papers and his analyses of his own dreams, which reflect feelings of guilt about the episode. A more detailed account of the whole affair is also provided by the present author in the introduction to that volume.

In February 1885, Freud applied for the post known in German as *Privatdozent*, roughly equivalent to lecturer, in neuropathology. The post allowed the holder to give lectures but not to attend faculty meetings. Neither was there a salary attached, but it was a highly prestigious appointment, and an application for such a post had to contain evidence of high level research. In March, Freud also applied to the faculty for a travel grant. It would not provide very much money and would only last for six months. His overriding purpose in applying for the grant was that it would enable him to travel to Paris and attend the lectures of the renowned Jean Martin Charcot. He had to wait till mid-June before both the appointment and the grant were confirmed. By the end of August, he had left the General Hospital. His immediate plan was to visit Martha for six weeks in Wandsbeck, where he endeavoured to overcome any final linger zing objections that her mother might have towards him as a future son-in-law. After this he would go on to Paris, where he arrived eventually in the middle of October 1885.

Hypnosis and Hysteria:
Charcot, Breuer and 'Anna O'
(1885–95)

Freud arrived in Paris on 13 October 1885 and stayed until 28 February 1886, though he did spend about nine days at Christmas with Martha's family in Wandsbek. For the first six weeks he lived in the Hôtel de la Paix, in an alley off the Rue Gay-Lussac in the Latin Quarter. When he went to Wandsbek on 20 December he had to give up this room and on his return he rented a room in the Hôtel de Brésil in the Rue de Goff. He found the crowds and complexity of the city bewildering when he first arrived, and wrote to Martha of how lonely and isolated he felt, but he gradually warmed to the city's charms and started sending her long evocative descriptions of its sights. He was to become a prolific writer of travel letters in his later years. He evoked for her the elegance of the Champs-Elysées, the quiet charm of the Tuileries and the bustle of the Place de la République. He also visited the Musée Cluny, Notre Dame and was greatly impressed by the Père Lachaise cemetery. In the Louvre he was particularly fascinated by the Egyptian antiquities, such as the bas-reliefs and the colossal statues of kings, as well as the huge figures of Assyrian kings with lions in their arms. This was a passion he was to maintain throughout his life, adding to his own collection of small ancient figurines whenever he could afford it.

In Paris Sigmund had only a little money for his everyday needs, and sought out the most modest restaurants, drinking cheap red wine. He did treat himself to the theatre occasionally, but then only to inexpensive seats which doubtless had restricted views. He improved his French by watching Molière comedies and could not resist seeing the famous Sarah Bernhardt. Perhaps to reassure his fiancée he wrote that French women were generally extremely ugly. The most far-reaching experience of his stay in Paris, however, was undoubtedly the time he spent studying under Charcot and getting to know the great man personally.

Jean Martin Charcot was at the height of his fame as the world's leading expert on neurology when Freud studied under him at the Salpêtrière clinic. He was a brilliant, charismatic man, who encouraged his students with great warmth and had a memorable, witty lecturing style. Years later in his 'Auto-biographical Study' Freud was to recall a pithy response of Charcot's which had stayed with him: '*La théorie, c'est bon, mais ça n'empêche pas d'exister*', which Strachey translated as 'Theory is all very well but it does not prevent [the facts] from existing.'[3] Strachey's phrase in parenthesis is a fairly free interpretation, and it might be better to replace it with an implied 'things'. Freud spent about six weeks studying children's brains in Charcot's pathology laboratory. This led later to extensive papers on cerebral paralysis and a work on aphasia. It was Charcot's theories on psychology which most intrigued him, however, and he wrote to Martha that no other human being had ever had such a great influence on his thinking. Charcot shared not only his convictions but also his doubts with his students, revealing openly his own hesitancy of formulation. It was a quality which was to become the hallmark of Freud's own mode of thought. Charcot also had the impressive skill of being able to discriminate finely, both between different types of illness which appeared closely related, and in general between physical and mental illnesses, at a time when most physicians often confused the two. Above all he took the odd and strange behaviour of many of his patients seriously. He considered hysteria to be a real disturbance which afflicted both men and women and not just a conscious ploy adopted to avoid responsibility. And for him hypnotism was not just a quasi-mystical procedure adopted by quacks but one that had a demonstrable mental effect. Freud witnessed him curing cases of hysterical paralysis by the use of hypnotic suggestion. The germ of Freud's later theory of transference is to be found in the evidence provided by the behaviour of some of Charcot's patients who, during and even after hypnosis, succumbed to a feeling of love and even erotic desire towards the hypnotist. While being impressed, however, Freud remained sceptical of Charcot's explanation of hypnosis, and his assertion that it could only be effective with hysterics. Hippolyte Bernheim, in Nancy, was arguing at around the same time that hypnosis had broader applications as it was primarily dependent on suggestion. The ideas of both men were to be very influential in Freud's development of psychoanalysis in the 1890s.

Freud's relationship with Charcot undoubtedly became closer with his agreement to translate a volume of the great man's lectures into German. Freud provided different accounts of how this came about. In his 'Autobiographical Study' he wrote that he had overheard Charcot express the wish that someone would translate the lectures into German, and that Freud had then written to him with an offer of his services. But he wrote to Martha that the idea had occurred to him without any prompting from Charcot. Whatever the truth of the matter, Freud gained Charcot's approval, translating in addition some of his lectures which had not yet even appeared in French. Partly as a result of this commitment Freud visited Charcot at his home several times, sometimes to discuss the translations, but on at least three occasions, in January and February 1886, as a guest at social functions. Freud was clearly very nervous at such events, partly because of his halting French. He dressed very formally and reported to Martha that he boosted his confidence by taking a dose of cocaine. Much of this socialising Freud found dull but the cocaine kept his spirits up. On the first occasion, 19 January, various distinguished scientists were present, but an Italian artist by the name of Tofano was also there, as was the son of writer Alphonse Daudet. The next such occasion was a huge event involving about forty or fifty people, of whom Freud knew very few. The third occasion proved to be an extremely enjoyable dinner party, attended not only by medical experts but also Tofano again and a well-known sculptor. Freud also met Alphonse Daudet himself and his wife. Amongst other people Freud met in Paris was an Austrian physician, Richetti, whom he had known in Vienna, and who turned up to attend some of Charcot's demonstrations. Freud was fond of telling an amusing story of how he, Richetti and Richetti's wife went to what they thought was a good restaurant but which turned out to be a high-class brothel.

Freud left Paris on 28 February 1886, stopping for a few weeks in Berlin on his return journey. Here he found the ideas of the neurologists somewhat disappointing after the inspirational Charcot, but he made some useful studies of children's diseases in Adolf Baginsky's clinic. The reason for his interest in this topic was that before he went to Paris he had been offered a post by the pediatrist Max Kassowitz as director of a new neurological department to be opened in the Institute for Children's Diseases in Vienna. In Berlin he also managed to find some free time to enjoy studying the Pergamon sculptures in the Royal Museum. Once back in Vienna he had to submit a report on his trip to the medical faculty, at Easter. In this he expounded Charcot's ideas and lamented the lack of enthusiasm for them in German-speaking lands. He stressed that the future lay in the study of neuroses. Those in authority who read this report were not best pleased with its findings.

Now that Freud was no longer at the General Hospital he advertised his services in the *Neue Freie Presse* as a consultant on nervous diseases. He continued to do some research in Meinert's laboratory, but was now concerned to make a living from seeing private patients. This was in large part because he was now determined to get married as soon as possible, but also because he felt that the medical establishment was very much opposed to the new ideas he was introducing. Even Meynert, who had long supported Freud, now decided to break with him. Apart from his meagre income, however, Martha also had a reasonable dowry, and various members of her family and some friends contributed considerable sums of money. A civil wedding ceremony finally took place in Wandsbek on 13 September 1886. But by Austrian law a religious ceremony was also required, and on 14 September therefore, Freud, as anti-religious as they come, after quickly learning the necessary Hebrew responses, was formally married according to Hebrew rites. He wasted little time in starting a family and on 16 October 1887 wrote to the Bernays in Wandsbek with details of his first-born daughter, Mathilde, named after the wife of Josef Breuer.

Two men were to be particularly influential in Freud's life and on his work in the next decade: the long-established friend and mentor, Josef Breuer, and Wilhelm Fliess, with whom Freud was to have probably the most intense male relationship of his life. It was through Breuer that Freud and Fliess met; on Breuer's advice, Fliess attended some of Freud's lectures on neurology. Essentially an ear, nose and throat specialist, he had come to Vienna from Berlin in the autumn of 1887 to further his studies. In the discussions they had he greatly impressed Freud, who made the first overtures in the friendship with a letter on 24 November 1887. Fliess responded warmly and sent a gift. Later Freud was to send him a photograph of himself at Fliess's request. Over the years the modes of address employed in their letters became ever more intimate. Apart from their shared scientific interests and attitudes, both having been schooled in the Helmholtz methodology and philosophy of science, they also shared many broader cultural interests. Freud recommended many works of literature to his friend, including those of Shakespeare, Kipling and Conrad Ferdinand Meyer.

During the early period of his friendship with Fliess, Freud was becoming more and more dissatisfied with the various methods employed in the treatment of neurotic patients. In his later 'Autobiographical Study', Freud would claim that he did little scientific work during the period from 1886 to 1891 and published almost nothing, being preoccupied with supporting his growing family. However, his first book was published in 1891, so he must therefore have spent at least part of that time conducting research for it. *On the Conception of the Aphasias: A Critical Study* is still an impressive review of the current theories about the group of speech disorders known as aphasias. At the time the prevailing view was that such disorders had physical origins, probably lesions in specific areas of the brain. Freud argued that this was to overestimate the role of physiological factors. He was thus already beginning to suggest the reality of psychological causes.

It must be here recorded that in the autumn of 1891 the Freuds moved to the home that will be forever associated with his name and has been converted into a museum: Berggasse 19. He was to stay here for the next forty-seven years. The apartment had the advantage of being more spacious for his growing family and was also much cheaper. A year later they were to rent three further rooms on the ground floor, which Freud used as his study, consulting and waiting rooms.

Freud was still employing hypnotic suggestion with many of his patients, though he was not fully convinced of the long-term usefulness of this method. Nevertheless he published a short account in 1892 of its successful use. In his correspondence with Fliess he was beginning to stress more the probable influence of sexual conflicts in the development of neuroses. A healthy sexual life was beginning to appear crucial to a normal psychological condition. These ideas were very much in Freud's mind while he was working on the book that he would eventually publish together with Breuer: *Studies in Hysteria*. The work on this book was to prove central to the development of psychoanalysis but also led to the breakdown of the long-standing relationship between the two men.

The idea that sexual factors played an important role in the aetiology of neuroses did not occur spontaneously to Freud. Already sometime in the early 1880s Breuer had remarked to him that the neurotic behaviour of patients was usually connected with what went on between the sheets in their marriage. He had also overheard Charcot stressing to an assistant that certain nervous disorders are invariably related to genital matters. There had been other such incidents, too, but flashes of insight are one thing; the determination to work such insights through to their logical conclusion is quite another. By 1895 Freud was clearly investigating closely the role of sexual factors in the development of anxiety neurosis.

Freud felt isolated in this work and needed the support of a sympathetic colleague. The obvious choice was Breuer, because this older colleague and friend had been the first to introduce Freud to the study of hysteria and had shown a sympathetic interest in the use of hypnotism. He set about trying to win Breuer over to further investigation of hysteria and wanted him to publish his findings in the case of the patient who became known as 'Anna O.', but Breuer was at first most reluctant to do so. Finally Freud realised that this reluctance derived from certain unexpected developments in the case which had caused extreme embarrassment to Breuer. Breuer had treated the woman (whose real name was Bertha and who was an old friend of Martha's) from December 1880 to June 1882. She was a very intelligent young woman who had developed many distressing symptoms, which proved to be related to the fatal illness of her father. Amongst other symptoms she suffered from paralysis in three limbs, a persistent nervous cough, refusal to eat food and problems in her speech and vision. She also manifested symptoms of a double personality, one part of her appearing quite normal and the other behaving like a naughty child. Breuer was brought in initially to treat her cough, and she developed the habit of telling him about her unpleasant experiences and hallucinations. She found that when she discussed the first appearance of certain symptoms they completely disappeared. Thus the patient herself discovered what she called 'the talking cure'. She produced so much interesting material that Breuer also tried hypnosis on her to probe even deeper. Ernest Jones has provided a detailed account of subsequent developments related to him personally by Freud.[4] It seems that Breuer had become obsessed with the case and talked about it at great length with his wife, also a close friend of Freud. His wife became bored and eventually jealous, becoming generally depressed and morose. When Breuer realised this he was shocked, and, partly from a sense of guilt at how involved he had become with the young woman, decided to terminate the treatment. 'Anna O.' was by now much better, but shortly after Breuer had informed her of his decision he was summoned back to her, only to find that her condition seemed to be as serious as ever. She was in a state of pseudocyesis (hysterical pregnancy) which she clearly associated with the treatment being given her by Breuer. He calmed her down through hypnosis, fled the house, and went off with his wife the next day to spend a second honeymoon in Venice. In the account which Breuer did eventually publish he also played down the fact that the young woman continued to suffer many relapses.

Freud attempted to persuade Breuer to publish details of the case by telling him of his own experience of a patient who had suddenly flung her arms affectionately around his neck. He reassured Breuer that such reactions were common as a form of transference in certain kinds of hysteria. He also cited a similar case he had been working on recently with a 'Frau Cäcilie'. Thus Breuer agreed to collaborate with Freud on the understanding that the theme of sexuality would not be emphasised. They first published together a paper entitled 'The Psychical Mechanism of Hysterical Symptoms' in 1893 and then, in 1895, the famous *Studies in Hysteria*. It contained a reprint of their paper, five case histories, a theoretical account by Breuer and an essay by Freud on psychotherapy. The first of the case histories included was that of 'Anna O.' The book was not exactly a best seller: 1,800 copies had been printed and over the next thirteen years only 626 were sold. By 1894 Freud and Breuer had decided to end their collaboration; this was mainly due to Breuer's refusal to accept the far-reaching conclusions about the role of sexuality which Freud was now advocating. From then on Freud became very critical in his comments on Breuer, especially in his letters to Fliess. By the spring of 1896 he was feeling especially antipathetic, and at about the same time he was becoming more emotionally involved with Fliess.

This is not to say that Freud did not continue to be very much involved with family affairs, and in his letters to Fliess he often reported items of news about his family. Of his daughter Anna, he wrote affectionately of her endearing aggressiveness, and he particularly relished Martin's amusing sayings and his early attempts at writing poetry. He also shared his concerns about the children's health with his friend. Another important member of the household, who has given many writers cause for groundless speculation over the years, was Freud's sister-in-law Minna Bernays. While he was engaged to Martha and she engaged to Ignaz Schönberg he had written very affectionate letters to her. In 1886 Schönberg had died unexpectedly of tuberculosis, and she became resigned to life as a spinster. She was plain and looked much older than her years. She was also the more intellectual of the two sisters, and known for being witty. Freud found her conversation stimulating. She visited the family frequently and finally moved in with them in the mid-1890s. Later, Freud was to tell his friend Marie Bonaparte that at that time the only people who understood and believed in his ideas were Fliess and Minna. Whatever the truth of the matter, it was a period when Freud suffered serious bouts of depression and various physical ailments, but it was also the period of the gradual emergence of the body of ideas most closely associated with his name, with the birth of psychoanalysis. The decision to undertake the painful process of self-analysis undoubtedly made him particularly vulnerable during this period, and it is against this background that one must view the remarkable fact of his growing emotional dependence on Fliess.

The Birth of Psychoanalysis: Fliess and Self-Analysis (1895–1902)

Freud destroyed all the letters which Fliess sent to him, but, much against Freud's wishes, his own letters to Fliess have been preserved. They reveal a great deal about his emotional state and intellectual preoccupations during the period when he was developing the fundamental tenets of psychoanalysis. Above all, it is clear that the theories were formulated after pursuing many lines of thought which proved to be erroneous and making assumptions which later could be seen to be ill-founded. In the letters he wrote much of his ideals and ambitions and also of his need for Fliess's friendship and support in his investigations. In return he also supported and encouraged his friend in his own research. Biographers have noted that in his friendship with Fliess Freud became more dependent on the close support of another man than he did at any other time in his life. Whatever a full psychological explanation of this fact may be, it is clear that, having decided to undertake an unflinching analysis of his own psychological constitution, Freud was making himself very vulnerable to self-doubts and questionings.

The first steps in self-analysis would seem to date from July 1895, when he first attempted to analyse one of his own dreams. From then on he wrote frequently to Fliess of these analyses. By July 1897, the occasional analyses had become a regular practice, and it is thus from here that the self-analysis can be dated. The first dream analysis is known to have been of what has become known as 'the dream of Irma's injection'. The original dream occurred during the night of 23–24 July 1895. He rated its interpretation very highly and made it a cornerstone of his dream theory, though he did not pursue the analysis of it as far as was possible. The reason was that it touched upon complex personal experiences that he did not wish to make public. This has led many critics to accuse him of a lack of complete honesty, but it was a form of discretion which he exercised also in the accounts of all of his case histories. The dream reveals associations with the guilt he felt in relation to his recommending the use of cocaine to his friend Fleischl. A translation by the present author of Freud's analysis of the dream is to be found in the companion volume of writings by Freud entitled *On Cocaine*.

A crucial event in Freud's life which clearly greatly disturbed him and probably made him aware of the necessity of self-analysis was the death of his father in October 1896, at the age of eighty. Freud was later to assert that it was this event which led him to write *The Interpretation of Dreams* (published with the date 1900, though it actually appeared in 1899). This most extensive of his works was thus written hand in hand with his self-analysis. In the preface he wrote for the second edition in 1908, he claimed that he only realised after writing the book how much it had been influenced by his father's death.

In the process of mutual support Freud lent more credence to Fliess's theories than close critical assessment would justify. Fliess's own specialism was in fact very narrow: ailments of the nose and throat. He also became obsessed with numbers in general and periodicity in particular. Later Freud was to mock Fliess's more absurd flights of fancy, but at the height of their friendship he seems to have been willing to suspend judgement and even entertain their likely validity. In his own mind he clearly endowed Fliess with the ideal qualities of sound judgement and powerful intellect. Freud often remarked later, to Jones amongst others, that he had learnt when young to check a tendency in himself to excessively speculate, but it was a quality which he actively encouraged in Fliess. It seems in retrospect that he was seeking justification for the imaginative formulations of psychoanalysis with which he would soon surprise the world. Thus he wrote to Fliess, on 8 December 1895, that with his own limited knowledge he felt he could not adequately discuss his friend's remarkable insights into sexual physiology. He encouraged him to publish his ideas, even if they were as yet only conjectures, because the world needed such people who had the courage to make hypotheses which could not yet be proved.[5]

For a long time Freud was writing to Fliess more than once a week, reporting in detail on the work with his patients and his attempts at formulating his theories in schematic form. They also met as frequently as they could, in Vienna and sometimes in Berlin. They preferred, however, to meet well away from their places of work for two or three days at a stretch. Such occasions Freud came to refer to as their 'congresses'. They met in Salzburg (August 1890), Munich (August 1894), Dresden (April 1896), and there followed other meetings at places such as Nuremberg, Breslau and Innsbruck, culminating in the final one at Achensee in the Tyrol (September 1900), after which they never met again. From the time when Freud's self-analysis had begun, during July 1897, the letters reveal that Freud looked forward to their meetings with a longing akin to that for a lovers' tryst. The process of self-analysis undoubtedly brought to the surface many disturbing and unpalatable facts about his own psychological developments and needs, and there is a direct causal relationship between the self-analysis and the extreme variations in his moods and general mental condition in this period. At times the letters to Fliess reveal elation and surging self-confidence but at others he has lost all confidence, and is full of self-doubts. Freud was only too aware that he himself was afflicted by debilitating neuroses at that time, and in a letter to Fliess on 7 July 1897, he hinted how deeply his relationship with his friend was involved in this condition.

One significant product of Freud's association with Fliess was the writing of what he hoped would be a theory of scientific psychology, what has become known as 'The Project'. The origins of this can be traced to the early spring of 1895. It was to be a kind of economics of mental functioning, the first formulations in fact of the general principles of mental dynamics which were to be central to psychoanalysis. Freud never finished 'The Project', but what remains of it reveals how much he was obsessed by developing a psychology based on principles of natural science, an essentially mechanistic view of the mind which he never completely abandoned.

One thesis which Freud did feel compelled to abandon was that of his so-called 'Seduction Theory'. According to this theory, all neuroses were the result of an adult's sexual abuse of a child. For some years in the mid-1890s Freud had firmly believed in the theory. In a paper on the neuro-psychoses of defence, published in 1896, Freud confirmed his adherence to it unequivocally; on 21 April of that year he proclaimed it openly in a lecture to the Society for Psychiatry and Neurology, but he reported to Fliess that the eminent Richard von Krafft-Ebing, who had been present, described his thesis as a scientific fairy tale. By the summer of 1897, however, Freud was beginning to have doubts about his Seduction Theory, and in a letter to Fliess of 21 September he revealed that he no longer believed in it. What he had accepted as revelations by his patients of actual seduction during childhood he now realised were mainly creations of their own imagination. He did not reject all such accounts as fantasies, but became less dogmatic on the issue. He did not express openly his rejection of the theory for at least another six years. It was a crucial perception in the development of psychoanalysis however, because it led him to the realisation that products, figments, of the imagination could be analysed and interpreted as distorted or disguised expressions of very real psychic disturbances.

Freud's self-analysis thus consisted of drawing associations with memories of his own childhood, particularly of his relationship to his father, and of regular analyses of his dreams. However, his theory of dream interpretation was based not solely on these analyses but also on comparisons with the dreams of his patients. He gradually realised that what at first had seemed to be his own unique psychological constitution had in fact universal validity. It was not only he who had been infatuated with his mother and jealous of his father's role in her affections. All male children went through the same stages of emotional development, and such a fact, he informed Fliess, might well explain the powerful effect of dramas such as *Oedipus Rex* and *Hamlet*. Thus was the Oedipus complex born.

One effect of Freud's self-analysis and his exploration of his own Oedipus complex was that he gradually understood more about the reasons for his dependence on Fliess, and this enabled him to overcome it. It also enabled him to perceive more clearly the inadequacies in Fliess's mode of scientific thinking. When the two friends met in the summer of 1900 at the Achensee they argued angrily, each criticising the other's work. Their differences had become irreconcilable, and, although they maintained some contact, they never met again.

It should not be imagined that during this period of intense self-exploration Freud shut himself off from normal human intercourse. It has already been noted that his correspondence with Fliess also contained many accounts of family events and the behaviour of his children. In 1895, for the sake of its congenial company, he joined the Jewish lodge known as the B'nai B'rith Society, of which he remained a member for the rest of his life. There were family visitors, too, including, in 1896, his half-brother Emanuel from England. He also relaxed occasionally with a game of chess or cards, including patience, and enjoyed meeting friends for a round of the old Viennese card game of Tarock. He would occasionally attend public lectures, such as one given by Mark Twain on 2 September 1898 in Vienna. When alone at home he gained enormous pleasure from his growing collection of antiquities, particularly Egyptian statuettes.

The 'congresses' with Fliess were not the only occasions on which Freud managed to get away from Vienna. There were more relaxing escapes every summer. By about mid-July every year he would relinquish his studies and spend the rest of the summer months with his family in some resort or other with scenic charms. He might well do some work during this time, but relaxing, walking and enjoying the local cuisine were of prime concern. He would then return to the serious business of work by mid-September. In the summer of 1890 the Freud family were in the Semmering area, then for four successive years in Reichenau. In 1895 they went to Bellevue, very close to Vienna. For the next three years they went to Obertressen, near the Alt-Aussee, and in 1899 came the first visit to Berchtesgaden in Bavaria. Using these locations as the family's summer base, Freud also undertook with various companions trips into Italy. It was in August of 1895 that he had his first glimpse of the country, when he spent a week with his brother Alexander in Venice. In 1896 he was again in Italy with Alexander, visiting Bologna, Venice again, Padua, Faenza and Ravenna, with a whole week in Florence. In 1897 he was in Venice yet again, as well as Pisa, Siena, San Gimignano, Chiusi, Orvieto, Arezzo and Perugia, and there were more Italian destinations in 1898. The family spent a large part of the summer of 1899 in a farmhouse near Berchtesgaden, with Freud joining them for only a short time at the end of June, spending his time there completing *The Interpretation of Dreams*. Whenever he was away on his travels he would write home to Martha and the family with evocative accounts of all that he had experienced. These travelogues provide a delightful counterpoint to his earnest psychological investigations.

While he was studying dreams Freud also recorded many examples of other kinds of mental functions and indeed mal-functions which he came to refer to as the psychopathology of everyday life: verbal and other mistakes such as mislaying objects; forgetting to carry out intentions; accidents which were not really accidents. His interest in such phenomena seems to date at least from late 1897, when he tried to analyse why he could not find an address in Berlin that he needed. By January 1901, he had completed the text of *The Psychopathology of Everyday Life*, which has become one of his most popular books. It is this book which introduced into the English language the notion of 'Freudian slips', the popular rendering of Freud's German term *'Fehlleistungen'*.

One other development in Freud's life during these years which deserves some attention is the process of his academic advancement. By January 1897, he had been a *Privatdozent* for twelve years, which was an exceptionally long time to remain at such a level. In February of that year he learned that a proposal had been put forward by two influential professors, Hermann Nothnagel and Richard von Krafft-Ebing, that he be nominated for the position of what Ernest Jones referred to as Associate Professor. The title in German is *Ausserordentlicher Professor*, which implies that the appointed person has exceptional or 'extra-ordinary' accomplishments. It was an appointment valued largely for prestige, because it carried no salary and no right of membership of any faculty council. The only other benefit was that it enabled the recipient to demand higher fees of patients. Freud was passed over for many years, and for a long time this did not matter to him. Then, in September 1901, his attitude changed. Many factors had contributed to this change of heart, not least the exhilaration he felt on first visiting Rome. He had been feeling depressed after the completion of his study of dreams and the less-than-enthusiastic reception it received. He was also worried about his financial situation. He had long wanted to visit Rome, but had also felt a strange inhibition about going there. In 1897 he actually had a dream that he and Fliess were planning to hold one of their 'congresses' in the city. He was well aware of the neurotic nature of his inhibition, and noted that hitherto he had only got as near to Rome as Hannibal, one of his boyhood heroes, had done. He also perceived oedipal

aspects of this neurosis, recalling the ancient oracular pro-
clamation to the Tarquins that the person who first kissed the
mother would become ruler of Rome. Finally, and probably
after realising the roots of his own inhibition, he took the plunge
and went to Rome in September 1901, in the company of his
brother Alexander. Here he visited all the usual tourist sights,
not failing to throw a coin into the Fontana di Trevi. It was
ancient and Renaissance Rome which fascinated him most. He
also spent some considerable time studying with admiration
Michelangelo's statue of Moses, to which he was later to devote
an entire essay, one of his few ventures into the analysis of works
of art. His letters home to Martha reveal how ecstatic the city
had made him feel.

On his return from Rome Freud found that he had even fewer
patients than before, and he realised that, for the sake of the
security of his family at least, he would have to take more active
steps to secure his academic advancement. This involved seeking
to persuade influential men to support his application, a procedure which was the norm but in which Freud had hitherto
been reluctant to become involved. First Nothnagel and Krafft-
Ebing would have to renew their proposals. A patient, who had
also become a friend, the Baroness Ferstel, used her influence
to obtain an interview with the Minister of Education. She
discreetly 'bribed' the minister with the donation of a work of
art for the gallery which he was establishing. There has been
much discussion about the extent to which the delay in Freud's
advancement was due to prejudice against him in official and
academic circles, and about whether this prejudice was predom-
inantly due to the nature of his ideas or the fact that he was a
Jew. It seems likely that both his emphasis on sexuality and his
Jewishness worked against him. Convincing arguments and
evidence on these points are provided by Peter Gay in his biography.[6] The honour was eventually bestowed and Freud had to
take part in an official ceremony in the presence of the Austrian
Emperor, on 22 February 1902. He viewed the proceedings with

ironical amusement, and he wrote, in his last letter to Fliess, that congratulations were raining down on him as though the Emperor had officially recognised the role of sexuality in the origin of neuroses.

Freud's appointment did indeed coincide with a gradual change in his fortunes. In Jones' words: 'He had become, if not respectable, at least respected.'[7] Freud took advantage of his right to give public lectures, which became very popular, and started to gain some international recognition. In 1901 he also occupied himself with writing up the famous case of 'Dora', and was collecting material for his later book on jokes and wit. He had started treating 'Dora', a girl of eighteen, in October 1900, but the treatment lasted only eleven weeks. The patient herself broke it off before the end of the year. He delayed publishing the case history, however, for reasons of discretion, and did not do so until April 1905, under the title rendered in English as *Fragment of an Analysis of a Case of Hysteria*.

After the seal of approval bestowed on him by the Emperor in February of 1902, Freud began to gather a small group of enthusiastic supporters around him, and it was then that the famous 'Wednesday Meetings' were established at his home in the Berggasse. They began with only five physicians in attendance but gradually expanded to include various interested laymen. At these regular meetings, which took place in Freud's waiting room, they discussed psychoanalytic theory in general, case studies and various other possible applications of psychoanalytic theory. Freud, of course, was always in the chair. The idea of such a regular meeting had been suggested to him by Wilhelm Stekel, who himself had conducted research into childhood sexuality, and was helped by Freud to overcome a neurotic problem he was suffering from. Two other early members of the 'Wednesday Meetings' were doctors who attended some of Freud's lectures: Max Kahane and Rudolf Reitler. Kahane worked in a sanatorium treating neurotics with traditional methods, and Reitler was one of the first after Freud to practise psychoanalysis. Another founder member, Alfred Adler, claimed that he had written a defence of Freud's views at that time in the *Neue Freie Presse*, but it has proved impossible to confirm this. Adler was a socialist and very much concerned about the social implications of Freud's theories. They decided to name their weekly meetings the 'Psychological Wednesday Society', and Stekel began to publish a report of their proceedings regularly in the Sunday edition of the *Neues Wiener Tagblatt*. The meetings settled into a regular format: first a member would read a paper; then there would be a pause while coffee and cakes were served, with a plentiful supply of cigarettes and cigars; and then a general discussion would follow. Freud was always allowed the last word.

In those early days of the society there was exuberance and enthusiasm every time its members came together. They reported that every gathering brought new intellectual stimulation and exciting insights. These meetings were also a great boost to Freud's self-confidence. After the break-up with Fliess it was just the kind of reassuring support that he needed. Disagreements and dissensions were still in the future, as were the partings of the ways with some of those followers Freud had believed most loyal. But that future was none too distant.

Recognition and Dissension: Breaking with Adler and Jung (1902–14)

In the first years after its founding the 'Psychological Wednesday Society' went from strength to strength, with new members joining either from personal recommendation or following attendance at Freud's lectures. Amongst others there were Alfred Meisl and Max Graf, whose son would be immortalised as 'Little Hans' in Freud's famous case history, and the man who would become Freud's publisher, Hugo Heller. The number of Freud's private patients had also increased, with the majority coming not from Vienna but from further east, from Russia, Poland, Hungary and other countries. The early years of the new century thus brought Freud some contentment and sense of fulfilment, and he was able to maintain a satisfying social and family life, culminating every week in a game of tarock on Saturday evening with his regular friends. The summer holidays also settled into a routine: in 1902, 1903 and 1904 the family spent the greater part of the summer at the Villa Sonnenfels near Berchtesgaden in Bavaria. In 1903 Sigmund took a short two-week trip with his sister-in-law, Minna Bernays. After a week in Munich and Nuremberg, where they found it too hot, they went to Bozen, seeking cool mountain air. Minna did not feel well and the weather was stormy, however, so they spent the rest of the trip at Meran.

In the following few years the membership of the 'Psychological Wednesday Society' steadily increased, admitting many members who would become significant thinkers in their own right. In 1903 Paul Federn joined; in 1905, Eduard Hitschmann. In 1906 Otto Rank joined on the recommendation of Adler, soon becoming the society's secretary and very much under Freud's wing. In 1907 Fritz Wittels, who would later write a biography of Freud, joined, with Victor Tausk joining in 1909 and Hanns Sachs in 1910, amongst many others. Ernest Jones has recorded that his first visit to the society was on 6 May 1908. Another significant member to join at about this time was Sándor Ferenczi, from Budapest. Just before Jones's visit the society changed its name to the 'Vienna Psychoanalytical Society'. The procedure involved dissolving the former society and reconstituting it. This was to enable those members who no longer had sympathy with Freud's ideas to resign without embarrassment or offence.

It was around this time that two of Freud's major and most well-known works also appeared, both in 1905: *Three Essays on the Theory of Sexuality* and what is usually translated as *Jokes and Their Relation to the Unconscious*. Not only did *Three Essays* sell well but Freud also came eventually to regard it as an accomplishment equal to *The Interpretation of Dreams*. Acceptance of its ideas became for Freud a way of testing the degree of a reader's commitment to the basic tenets of psychoanalysis.

There were also frequent guests who participated informally in the Wednesday meetings, many of whom later became formal members. Among these was Karl Abraham from Berlin, with whom Freud was to conduct a lengthy correspondence. It was in this way that psychoanalysis gradually became internationalised. Freud was particularly pleased at the interest shown by leading Swiss psychiatrists, such as Max Eitingon, Ludwig Binswanger and the man whom Freud came to consider his natural heir or 'crown prince', Carl G. Jung. Apart from Ernest Jones, another English-speaking visitor was the American A.A. Brill, who would become one of Freud's main translators. The founder of psychoanalysis in Italy, Edoardo Weiss, also paid a visit.

Apart from supporters among the medical professions Freud was also pleased to discover enthusiastic adherents among intelligent laymen. Two personalities stand out especially in this respect and with both he was to conduct extensive correspondence: the Swiss pastor Oskar Pfister, and the woman of letters and friend of poets and philosophers Lou Andreas-Salomé.

In many respects Pfister was a most unlikely man to become not only an adherent of psychoanalysis but also a close friend of Freud's. He was a Protestant pastor, born in Zürich in 1837, and Freud, of course, was an atheist Jew. But Pfister had long come to detest the obsession amongst theologians with debating definitions and meanings of words. For him the first duty of a man of religion was to help people in distress; long before he read any of Freud's works he had started studying psychology, but the theses propounded by the theorists he consulted failed to convince him. Then he discovered the writings of Freud, which provided him with what he had been searching for: a way of analysing the depths of the human soul. It was Pfister who initiated the friendship by sending Freud a paper he had written on suicide among schoolboys. Many of Freud's associates were dubious about Pfister's approach to psychoanalysis, but Freud defended him. He also welcomed him into his home, the first visit being in April 1909. He won the hearts of Freud's family by showing sincere interest in all its members, unlike most of his colleagues who only maintained a polite show of cordiality, their real interest being in the subsequent intellectual discussion with Sigmund. Pfister later risked losing his parish because of his involvement with Freud, but Freud's support gave him the strength to continue. His knowledge of psychoanalysis undoubtedly helped him in his pastoral duties, and the two friends openly discussed their differences over religion in their correspondence.

Lou Andreas-Salomé and Oskar Pfister were poles apart. She was a beautiful and sensuous woman who had been an intimate friend of the philosopher Friedrich Nietzsche in the 1880s and later was also a close friend of the poet Rainer Maria Rilke.

In 1887 she married Friedrich Carl Andreas, a specialist in oriental studies at the University of Göttingen. Marriage did not prevent her from conducting many affairs, however, especially with illustrious men. She was an extremely intelligent woman who impressed with her acute understanding of psychoanalytic theory. She first met Freud at the congress of psychoanalysts in Weimar in 1911, and in the autumn of 1912 she went to Vienna to study psychoanalysis. Freud was greatly impressed by her intellectual powers. While in Vienna she attended the Wednesday meetings, but not all her preoccupations in the city were of an intellectual nature: it seems likely that she had a brief affair with handsome young Viktor Tausk. She became a regular guest in Freud's home, and, after her return to Göttingen, they maintained a long-lasting correspondence.

Freud appreciated such supportive friendships, especially at a time when there was much opposition to and criticism of his theories, some of it crude and tasteless and revealing ignorance of his actual work. The implication was often that Freud's writings were pornographic and not worthy of serious scientific consideration. It is in the light of such common misrepresentation of his ideas that one must see his concern to maintain a hard core of loyal supporters around him. And after getting to know Carl Jung he began to feel that the future of psychoanalysis was assured in Jung's hands.

The association with Jung started in April 1906, when Jung sent Freud a copy of a volume which he had edited and contributed entitled *Diagnostic Association Studies*. He was born in a village near Lake Constance in Switzerland as the son of a pastor. From his early childhood he had been obsessed by his own haunting and mysterious dreams. He was essentially an introverted person but could surprise by occasional extroverted behaviour, and was a man of frequently changing moods. He studied medicine at the University of Basel but always maintained a fascination for the mystical aspects of religion and for the occult in general. In 1900 he joined the famous Burghölzli sanatorium, the psychiatric clinic of the University of Zürich with the famous Eugen Bleuler as its director, who had, like Freud, studied with Charcot in Paris. Jung became familiar with Freud's dream theory by being asked by Bleuler to write a report on it for his staff. He rapidly became an ardent adherent of psychoanalysis. From early on, however, he expressed doubts about the central role which Freud attributed to early experiences in the young. At the birth of their relationship therefore could also be found the seeds of its dissolution.

It has been remarked upon by other biographers that Freud idealised Jung at first in a way uncannily similar to the way in which he had earlier treated Fliess, though now he was more aware of the process that was taking place within himself. He openly admitted his fondness for Jung but also wrote to him that he had learned to suppress that aspect of what psychologists at that time commonly called the psyche. A whole year passed before they were able to meet for the first time, in March 1907. Jung, together with his wife and a younger colleague, Ludwig Binswanger, visited Freud at his home. Jung recalled later that they talked for about thirteen hours, almost non-stop. Subsequently they wrote supportive and encouraging letters to each other. Jung's criticisms seemed for a while to be stilled. Yet his doubts never truly died down, and there was always an insecure element in their relationship, with Jung being frequently jealous of Freud's praise of other psychoanalysts.

At the end of 1907 there were some changes to Freud's domestic arrangements. His sister, Rosa, decided to give up her flat which was opposite Freud's on the same landing of the house. Freud took this opportunity to acquire more spacious accommodation for himself, and he gave up the much smaller flat on the ground floor where had lived and worked for about fifteen years. Unfortunately for biographers he also took the opportunity to destroy many of his private papers.

On 4 March 1908, Freud decided, after living in Vienna for about fifty years, to take up official citizenship of the city. This was undoubtedly not out of any growing emotional attachment to his place of work, but in all probability to enable him to vote in local elections should he so desire. In the summer of that year the family spent their holiday near Berchtesgaden again, with Freud staying there for part of the time in the company of Sandor Ferenczi. On 1 September he set off for England to visit his half-brother Emanuel. He travelled via the Hook of Holland and Harwich in England, but made a point of breaking his journey in The Hague to look at the Rembrandt collection there. He had not seen England since his first visit at the age of nineteen. On this occasion he spent a fortnight there, travelling around with Emanuel to visit such places as Southport, Blackpool and St Anne's on the Lancashire coast. By 7 September he was back in Manchester, meeting up with his other half-brother Philipp, going on alone to London the same evening. While in London he indulged himself, buying a pipe and some cigars, and saw some of the sights, most memorable to him being a visit to the British Museum to study the Egyptian antiquities, amongst other items. He spent his last day in London looking at the Gainsboroughs and Reynolds in the National Gallery. Then, on 15 September, he set off for Harwich where he met up with Emanuel again. They went to Berlin together, with Freud leaving only one day later for Zürich. Here he was the guest of the Jungs for four days, during which time Jung took him on a tour by car to the Rigi and Mount Pilatus. The relationship seems to have been at its warmest and most trusting at this time. On 21 September Freud took the overnight train to Milan, changing trains there for Besenzano, where he met up with Minna. They spent a few days together in Salo on Lake Garda, travelling home eventually via Bozen and arriving in Vienna on 29 September.

Amongst papers on anal eroticism, sexual morality and bisexuality Freud also published in 1908 a short essay normally translated as *Creative Writers and Daydreaming*, in which he reflected on how writers modify their own fantasies through their work into forms of expression which are acceptable to the public. The work is often cited as evidence of Freud's reductive views on art in general but it must be interpreted in the context of his theory of mental functions as a whole.

In December of that same year Freud received a surprise invitation. Stanley Hall, the President of Clark University in Worcester, Massachusetts, asked him to come and give a course of lectures as part of the twentieth anniversary celebrations of the university. It was to be an all expenses paid trip, but Freud felt he had to decline because the date proposed, in July, would mean he would have to neglect his practice for three weeks altogether. But after a few months Hall renewed the invitation, explaining that they had had to postpone the celebrations in any case until September. Freud accepted this time and Ferenczi agreed to go with him. Freud could not work up very much enthusiasm for America, however, finding that only two things really interested him: the prospect of being able to see a collection of Cypriot antiquities which was kept in New York, and the chance to see Niagara Falls. The final plan was to travel from Bremen on the *George Washington*, a Nordeutscher Lloyd ship, on 21 August. In June, Jung informed Freud that he had also been invited to the event, so they decided to travel together.

On 7 February 1909 an important Freud family event took place, with Sigmund's eldest daughter Mathilde marrying Robert Hollitscher, a thirty-three year old Viennese businessman. Sigmund had hoped she would marry Ferenczi.

In the summer of that year the family stayed in Ammerwald, in North Tyrol, near the Bavarian Alps. In order to make his way to Bremen Freud had to leave on 19 August, travelling via Oberammergau and Munich to Bremen where he met up with Ferenczi and Jung. While having lunch there a strange incident occurred. The three men were drinking wine together, Freud having just managed to persuade Jung to have a glass despite the latter's professed abstinence. Suddenly Freud fainted and fell down. It seems that there might have been some psychological cause of this incident. Jung had been talking at great length about the ongoing excavation of prehistoric remains in an area of Northern Germany. Because Jung was so persistent in discussing the topic of death and human remains Freud interpreted it as concealing a death wish against him. The fear of this possibility probably caused Freud to faint. Whatever Jung's actual feelings might have been, it is clear that Freud was still extremely sensitive to the possibility of Jung's usurping his authority. On the 21st they travelled from Bremen as planned via Southampton.

On board ship Freud attempted to keep a diary but gave up and started writing letters to his wife instead. It seems that the three colleagues spent a lot of their spare time analysing each other's dreams. One highlight of the crossing for Freud was discovering that his cabin steward was reading *The Psychology of Everyday Life*.

They had about a week to see something of New York, staying at the Hotel Manhattan; Ernest Jones came down from Toronto to join up with A.A. Brill, both acting as guides for their colleagues. Amongst other sights they visited Central Park, Chinatown and the Jewish Quarter and spent an afternoon in Coney Island, which Freud found to be just a larger version of the Prater in Vienna. On their second day they visited the Metropolitan Museum, where Freud was most interested to view the Grecian antiquities. On the following day Freud was able, for the first time in his life, to see a film, which seems to have provided him with some amusement if little more. On 4 September they left for New Haven by boat and then went on by train to Boston and Worcester.

Remarkably, Freud seems not to have prepared for his lectures in any way and professed to not having the faintest idea what he was going to talk about. Jung suggested that he concentrate on the dream theory, but he finally agreed to provide a general introduction to psychoanalysis. The actual content he worked out in morning strolls with Ferenczi on the day of delivery. The five lectures he delivered in German and his general tone and style was warmly received. The famous psychologist and philosopher, William James, made a special trip to Worcester to hear him and he and Freud took a walk together. In his later autobiographical essay Freud recalled how James had suddenly stopped, asked Freud to hold his briefcase and walk on, assuring him that he would rejoin him later: he had felt the onset of an attack of angina. A year later James was to die of the same condition. While James had his doubts about Freud's theories, believing as he did that religion could provide a higher level of truth, he nevertheless respected his findings in psychology. Naturally enough James found that he was more drawn to the ideas of Jung, who had a more sympathetic attitude to religion.

After delivering the Clark Lectures, Freud, Jung and Ferenczi visited Niagara Falls, taking a trip in the *Maid of the Mist* and setting foot briefly in Canada. They then spent several days with the Harvard neurologist, James Putnam, in the Adirondacks. Here the most memorable events were Jung's regaling the company with German songs and Freud's sighting of a wild porcupine. Before setting off on the trip to America, Freud had declared that to avoid extreme disappointment at the outcome of the trip he had decided to consider the lectures as only a secondary goal, with the sighting of a wild porcupine as his primary aim in going to America. Then, after two more days in New York, they sailed back to Bremen on the *Kaiser Wilhelm der Grosse* on 21 September. Freud did not leave America with very favourable impressions, and, although he appreciated the growth of his following there, he retained throughout his life a lack of sympathy for things American, often commenting on its culture in a sarcastic vein.

Back in Vienna Freud found himself rather exasperated by his old Viennese followers, and he criticised them in no uncertain terms in his correspondence with Jung. His criticism seems not to have been misplaced because soon he would have to deal with the dissensions of two of his long-time supporters: Alfred Adler and Wilhelm Stekel. For a long time Freud got on well with Adler, and although they disagreed about some of Adler's terminology, Freud respected him intellectually. But Adler's stress on the role of heredity and physiological factors in the origins of neuroses was to distance him gradually from Freud. The first real confrontation between the two men and with Jung's supporters occurred at the International Congress of Psychoanalysts in Nuremberg in the spring of 1910.

At the Nuremberg congress Ferenczi angered the Viennese members by putting forward Freud's proposals for an essentially Swiss leadership of the planned International Psychoanalytical Association and adding some criticisms himself of the Viennese circle. In a small private meeting with his Viennese colleagues Freud argued that it was crucial that the movement be perceived as being truly international and not dominated by Viennese Jews. Finally a compromise was reached which seemed to satisfy all: Jung would only be president for a limited term of two years. In April, after the congress, at a meeting of the Vienna Psychoanalytic Society, Freud attempted to smooth the ruffled feathers of his colleagues by nominating Adler to take over his role as presiding official and set up a new journal, the *Zentralblatt für Psychoanalyse*, which would be edited jointly by Stekel and Adler.

The crisis with Adler came to a head in November 1910, when Eduard Hitschmann proposed that Adler present an extensive account of his ideas for discussion by the society. Adler was only too willing and read two papers in January and February of 1911. The second of the two papers, entitled 'Masculine Protest as the Core Problem of Neurosis', revealed clearly that his ideas were no longer compatible with Freud's, and Freud responded with a devastating critique. Others present endeavoured to play down the differences, but for Freud Adler was redefining all the basic concepts of psychoanalysis and presenting them in an utterly different guise. By late February of 1911 it became clear that the fundamental differences necessitated Adler giving up his presiding role in the Vienna Psychoanalytic Society, and Stekel, who was then vice-president, followed suit. By June Freud had also persuaded Adler to give up his editorship of the new periodical, with Stekel staying on for some time. When the society met again after the summer recess Freud, who had told Ferenczi in advance of his intention, announced that Adler and his supporters had resigned and established a separate group which he considered hostile in nature. Altogether six supporters of Adler were forced to resign, with only Stekel staying on. Getting rid of Stekel would take a little longer.

Stekel had long been a problematic member of the society for reasons other than his adherence to Adler. There was no doubt that he was a talented analyst, and had provided some impressive insights, but he was at times irresponsible in his presentation of evidence. He would frequently, at the regular meetings, 'invent' a case which he claimed just to have experienced, and as his colleagues became aware of this idiosyncrasy of his, it became a standing joke to talk of Stekel's 'Wednesday patient'. Once, when presenting a paper on the psychological significance of surnames, Freud asked how Stekel could be so indiscreet as to quote the names of his patients, to which Stekel replied that he had made them all up. The occasion of the final break was an argument between Stekel and Tausk, whom Freud wanted to organise the review section of the *Zentralblatt*. Stekel refused to let Tausk contribute in any way to the periodical. As a result of this Freud persuaded almost all other members to withdraw from participation in the *Zentralblatt*. This led to Stekel's resignation from the society on 6 November. He continued to be the editor of the periodical, but its sales dropped rapidly and it eventually ceased publication after a few years.

While Freud was dealing with the crises with Adler and Stekel, matters were also not faring well with Jung. With Jung the break was much more radical and more painful. Despite Abraham's constant warnings to Freud that Jung was becoming too much involved in occult and mystical speculations, Freud preferred not to contemplate these facts, because of his high hopes that Jung would be his successor as leader of the movement. Jung himself reported that his dissension from Freud's ideas started during their trip to America together.[8] Certainly, during a session of mutual dream analysis on the voyage out, Freud had alienated Jung by his refusal to reveal some details of his private life, with the justification that it would put his authority at risk. Jung interpreted this as meaning that for Freud personal authority was more important than truth. In Freud's defence it could be argued that he was likely to be thinking of moral rather than professional authority. Whatever interpretation one puts on the event, it was clearly decisive for Jung.

Late in 1909 Jung had made it quite clear to Freud that he wanted to devote himself to a thorough study of mythology, which Freud encouraged, though warning him against too broad and diffuse a study. More and more, Jung preferred not to emphasise sexual factors in his psychological theories. In June 1910, Freud read a draft of the first part of Jung's essay 'Symbols of the Libido' and sent him a letter with both criticism and praise. It was in the second part of the essay that the divergence of their ideas was to become clear. By May 1911, Jung informed Freud that he had developed a different concept of libido, which he conceived as a more general tension, or mental energy. In the second part of the essay Jung also expressed the opinion that the idea of incest was not to be taken literally but should be understood as functioning symbolically. At this time Freud himself was becoming interested in broader cultural themes and was researching in fields which would eventually lead to the publication of *Totem and Taboo*. In early 1912 he and Jung found themselves disagreeing vehemently about the nature and meaning of the incest taboo. As is often the case with break-ups in relationships the final impetus came from essentially trivial misunderstandings. In April that year Freud became alarmed at the news that Ludwig Binswanger, then director of the sanatorium in Kreuzlingen, Lake Constance, had had to undergo an operation for a malignant tumour. He made a special visit to Binswanger, who asked Freud to keep the matter confidential. Jung's house was only forty miles away from Kreuzlingen in Küsnacht, but Freud, partially perhaps because he was pressed for time, and partially because Binswanger did not want his condition known and it would thus be difficult for Freud to explain his visit otherwise, decided not to visit Jung. When Jung learned that Freud had not taken the opportunity to call on him he was deeply offended, and subsequently referred to Freud's 'Kreuzlingen gesture' as an indication that Freud disapproved of the way that Jung was developing his ideas more independently.

Freud and those closest to him in the movement were clearly feeling extreme unease about their ability to retain the coherence of psychoanalysis as a movement. And in June 1912, while Ernest Jones was visiting Vienna, he had the idea of forming a secret committee of analysts loyal to Freud. His idea was that they would share ideas and news with each other in strictest privacy and agree to discuss together any inclination that any of them might have to question or distance themselves from the basic tenets of psychoanalysis. Rank and Ferenczi immediately agreed, and Freud was very enthusiastic. He suggested that Abraham and Sachs should also be members of such a committee. He was also very much aware of the romantic schoolboy nature of the enterprise, but it gave him enormous reassurance that some positive steps were being taken to safeguard the future of psychoanalysis.

In September Jung went to New York to give a course of lectures, and the reports which reached Freud indicated that Jung was taking an antagonistic attitude towards his theories. On his return, despite the enthusiastic account which Jung sent him, Freud could not be reassured, and while he did not fear complete separation, he no longer felt that they could maintain the same level of personal relationship. Then in November they met in Munich. The purpose of the meeting was essentially to found a new periodical to replace Stekel's *Zentralblatt*. In a long two-hour walk together before lunch Freud and Jung attempted to clear up the misunderstanding about the 'Kreuzlingen gesture'. It all centred on Jung not having checked that the letter in which Freud informed him of his visit had in fact been sent before the event.

It seemed to Freud that the matter had been settled, but there was then an odd occurrence. Freud suffered another fainting attack in very similar circumstances to the one in Bremen three years previously, which had also been in Jung's company. This one also occurred at the end of lunch after a lively discussion between Freud and Jung. Freud was annoyed that articles on psychoanalysis had been published in Swiss journals without mentioning his name. Suddenly Freud fell down in a faint, and Jung carried him to a couch, where he quickly revived. Whatever physical causes there may have been, Freud was later convinced that some unresolved element of his relationship with Fliess was involved in causing him to faint. For some time after this Freud and Jung continued to correspond, but the letters reveal many points of disagreement, especially over the relationship between Jung's ideas and those of Adler. By early January 1913, Freud suggested that, while it would be necessary to continue to communicate on business matters, they should discontinue their personal correspondence.

In August 1913, Jung gave some lectures in London in which he explicitly declared his intention to free psychoanalysis from its emphasis on sexuality, and he started to use the alternative name of 'analytical psychology' for his own theories. Despite their fundamental differences Freud attempted to continue working with Jung, and duly attended the International Congress of Psychoanalysts in Munich in September 1913. The vote on Jung's re-election as president was accompanied by general discontent and protest, with twenty people abstaining. Bad feelings continued to dominate working relationships well into the following year. In October 1913 Jung resigned from his role in the new periodical, the *Jahrbuch*, citing personal reasons. Freud suspected that he might nevertheless try to regain control of it. He was also anxious that Jung was still president of the international organisation. While working hard to ensure that both periodical and organisation remained in sympathetic hands, Freud was also pouring his anger into a work entitled 'History of the Psychoanalytic Movement', which, as he reported to Ferenczi in early November 1913, would contain a vehement critique of its dissenters. By the early spring of 1914, Freud had achieved one longed-for goal: on 20 April Jung resigned as President of the International Psychoanalytic Association. Then, in July, Freud's 'History' was published, which clearly and publicly separated the sheep from the goats. Being a psychoanalyst could now be seen to imply acceptance of the main tenets as laid down by Freud. This did not imply that disagreement over matters of theory or practical technique led to exclusion from some inner circle, however. Many independent thinkers who took issue with Freud over key principles remained lifelong friends, as was the case with Paul Federn, Ludwig Binswanger and Ernest Jones, amongst others.

Despite the stresses, strains and dissensions within the psychoanalytic movement in 1913 and 1914, Freud enjoyed periods of relaxation and pleasure with members of his family. After the international congress in 1913 he went to Rome with his sister-in-law, Minna, who joined him in the train from Bologna. He described spending seventeen very enjoyable days there, rediscovering old haunts and exploring new ones, but also managing to do some work, writing a preface for *Totem and Taboo* and working on a long study on narcissism. At Christmas he managed to travel to Hamburg to visit his daughter Sophie, leaving Vienna on 24 December and returning on the 29th. Early in 1914 Sophie was to have Freud's first grandson. He broke his journey in Berlin on Christmas Day, where he met up with his sister Marie and also contacted Abraham and Eitingon. Then, in June 1914, he went to Budapest for a few days with Rank, to attend the wedding of an ex-patient.

It was in June also that 'On Narcissism' was published in the *Jahrbuch*, and Freud started to feel that he could make firm plans for the family summer. But, on 28 June, international political events intervened in the personal and professional concerns of everyone in Europe: the Archduke Franz Ferdinand of Austria, heir to the throne, was assassinated by a Bosnian Serb in Sarajevo. In a letter to Ferenczi on that day Freud hinted darkly at as yet unforeseeable consequences to that deed.

War, Hardship and the Onset of Cancer (1914–23)

Immediately after the assassination of Archduke Franz Ferdinand it seemed as though Europe held its breath, fearful that some further awful catastrophe would follow but unsure exactly what that might be. Freud was no less fearful than others, but after weeks when none of the governments involved took any decisive steps, he decided to proceed with some of his family plans, allowing his youngest daughter, Anna, to travel to Hamburg on 7 July and on to England on 18 July. He also left Vienna himself at about the same time for Karlsbad, inviting Eitingon and his wife to join him there early in August. Only a few days later, on 23 July, the Austrian government delivered an ultimatum to Serbia, which however agreed only partially to its terms. Austria promptly declared war and bombarded Belgrade. By early August most of Europe had been brought into the conflict. In late July Freud clearly believed that there was still some hope that the conflict would not spread. He wrote to Abraham on 26 July expressing the wish, at least, that the war might remain restricted to the Balkans. By the 29th he was even more optimistic, wondering whether within a matter of weeks the world might feel rather ashamed at all the unnecessary excitement, though he still entertained a lurking suspicion that some significant historical event was in the offing. When Britain finally joined in the war on 4 August, after Germany had failed to heed its warning, Freud found that the hostilities had divided his family. With Britain on the side of Russia and France against Germany and Austria, Anna and his other relatives in London were now in enemy territory.

Like many other Austrians at the time Freud felt relief when the period of uncertainty and tension broke and initially he shared some enthusiasm for the Austrian cause. He also regretted that Britain had entered the war on the wrong side. For a while it was difficult to concentrate on his psychoanalytical work and he spent a lot of time discussing the political events with his brother Alexander. He had few patients at the time but he was required to write out certificates for some to confirm that they were unfit for military conscription. He was not too keen on doing this and felt that they also had a duty to help the common cause, believing that fighting for their country might actually do them a lot of good. Freud's enthusiasm lasted barely a few weeks however. He became generally disappointed with the way the Austrians were conducting the campaign against Serbia, and saw his country's only hope in the support provided by Germany. It now no longer seemed to him that the hostilities would be of only short duration.

The rest of Freud's plans for that summer were destined not to be fulfilled. He had intended to go on from Karlsbad to the Dolomites for a holiday, to Dresden for the congress in September, and thence to Leyden in Holland to deliver a lecture. However the political situation made him decide to return to Vienna on 5 August via Munich. Also in August his eldest son, Martin, then in Salzburg, volunteered for the army and became a gunner. He was sent for training in Innsbruck, where Freud went to visit him early in September. His youngest son, Ernst, would eventually volunteer and serve on the Italian front, but his second son, Oliver, would be rejected for service until 1916. In the third week of August, Anna, with the help of Ernest Jones, had managed to get back to Vienna, travelling via Gibraltar and Genoa in the company of the Austrian ambassador. Freud had not spent August in Vienna for thirty years and, having no pressing commitments, he spent much of the time studying and writing a description of his collection of antiquities.

It proved increasingly difficult to continue with the normal activities of the Vienna Psychoanalytic Society, and the international congress planned for Dresden in September had to be cancelled. Many of Freud's fellow psychoanalysts were also being conscripted. As doctors they were considered crucial for the war effort. Abraham was called up and sent to a surgical unit near Berlin; Ferenczi was dispatched to the provinces to join a regiment of Hungarian hussars. None of them were in any imminent danger, however, and could cope with the boredom of their duties by continuing with some writing at least.

Despite the dangers Freud decided to visit his daughter Sophie in Hamburg and set off for a twelve-day trip on 16 September. On the return journey he managed to meet up with Abraham in Berlin for five hours. It would be four years before they could meet again. On the 30th Ferenczi came to Vienna for analysis with Freud, but was only able to stay for three weeks before he was conscripted. By October Freud had resumed seeing patients, but he only had two, and by November he had only one. The extra time enabled him to write up his famous case history of the so-called 'Wolfman', which would not be published until four years later. On 11 November he wrote to Ferenczi that he had just heard of the death of his half-brother Emanuel in a railway accident. It must have distressed him greatly as they had been close since his childhood.

Freud's correspondence reveals that he was feeling generally depressed during December. He wrote to Abraham, for example, that he had always hated the thought of being poor and helpless to change his situation, but now that condition seemed to be fast approaching. He enjoyed his correspondence with Lou Andreas-Salomé during this period, however, for its uplifting effect. He found her optimism moving, though he could not help believing that the war had proved only too clearly the validity of the findings of psychoanalysis about human nature. On

Christmas Day he wrote to Ernest Jones summing up his feelings about the general situation and the prospects for the future. He felt that all they could do was 'keep a glow of fire going' until it could blaze up again. Their association was not alone in being unable to function in a truly international mode any more. He had no doubts about the survival of psychoanalysis in the long term; it was its short-term fate which worried him.[9]

At the beginning of the New Year in 1915 Freud's spirits improved with Germany's victories against Russia, and he was hopeful that peace might not be so far off, though he believed that it might be at the cost of Austria ceding land to Italy, which would necessitate the family travelling abroad on their future visits to San Martino. Naturally enough the family was generally anxious about the fates of the two sons who had enlisted. Martin was fighting in Galicia and Russia and, after Italy entered the war in April, Ernst was fighting there. Oliver was needed as an engineer and escaped direct confrontation with the enemy. During this time Freud was also endeavouring to ensure the continuation of the two psychoanalytic journals, *Imago* and the *Zeitschrift*, which he managed by publishing chapters from a forthcoming book in them. But the *Jahrbuch* would never appear again. He lost an important aide when Rank was called up in June.

After the outbreak of war it had not been possible to maintain the regular Wednesday meetings, but eventually they were resumed at less regular intervals and took place about every three weeks. One of the problems was the growing difficulty of travel, so that Freud had fewer visitors than usual for several years, with the exception of Ferenczi, who managed occasional brief visits. One notable visitor in that year was the poet Rainer Maria Rilke who spent an enjoyable evening with Freud's family. Surprisingly Freud did manage to fit in a considerable amount of travelling in the summer months. On 3 July he informed Abraham that he had just come back from a trip of a few days to Berchtesgaden where he had been looking at a house, having come to like the area after staying there during the previous three summers. On 17 July he went to Karlsbad again, which was particularly enjoyable due to the absence of large numbers of guests. On 12 August he returned to Berchtesgaden, so that he could travel easily to Ischl to visit his mother who would soon be eighty. On 13 September he went to Hamburg, via Munich and Berlin, in order to visit Sophie and see his first grandchild. Two weeks after this, as Abraham was now doing his military service, he went to see Frau Abraham and the children in Berlin and thence returned to Vienna. In the autumn he was to begin his series of public lectures on Saturday evenings at the university, introducing doctors and laymen to the basic principles of psychoanalysis. His intention from the start was eventually to publish them.

Despite the fact that there were often long delays in the post Freud did manage to maintain a considerable correspondence, even with Abraham who had been transferred to a distant part of East Prussia. The two men discussed Freud's developing ideas about the nature of melancholy and repression. Feeling that at sixty he might not have much longer to live, Sigmund worked on synthesising his ideas. He informed his followers of his intention to write a series of essays which would be published in book form after the war was over, and bear a title indicating its focus on what he termed 'metapsychology'. By this he meant a comprehensive account of all the interrelated functions of the mental processes. By early August 1915 he was able to report to Jones that all twelve of the essays were almost completed. Perhaps the most well-known of them are 'Instincts and their Vicissitudes', 'The Unconscious', 'The Metapsychological Supplement to the Theory of Dreams' and 'Mourning and Melancholia'. The remaining seven essays were completed but Freud later destroyed the manuscripts. It is not clear why he took this action, and one must assume that he subsequently modified the ideas expressed in them. Four other papers were published in 1915, the most popular of which proved to be 'Some Character-Types Met with in Psychoanalytic Work' and 'Thoughts for the Times on War and Death'.

In a letter to Eitingon on New Year's Day 1916, Freud reported that Martin was now a lieutenant, Ernst a cadet and that both were serving on the Italian front. Oliver was busy building a tunnel under the Carpathian Mountains. There was, however, a big disappointment in store for Freud in January 1916: Rank was transferred to Cracow, and, apart from a brief trip to Constantinople in August, he would remain there for the rest of the war. Freud depended on him for help with his editorial work and the publishing process. He had no one else to help him but Sachs, who fortunately was able to step into Rank's shoes.

In February Freud's health was not at its best: he suffered a serious bout of influenza and there were signs of trouble with his prostate. In May it was his sixtieth birthday and he bemoaned the fact that news of his maladies had spread to the public through newspaper reports. The result was that he had to spend much time writing thank-you letters. In June, Ferenczi came to Vienna again for three weeks to continue Freud's analysis of him, but then was yet again interrupted by having to return to his military duties. Abraham attempted to arrange a congress in Munich for September of that year but the closure of the frontier between Austria and Germany provided too many difficulties. It also meant that Freud could not go to Berchtesgaden that summer, nor could he visit his daughter in Hamburg. Instead he left for Bad Gastein on 16 July, but after a week he went on to Salzburg, staying for five weeks in the Hotel Bristol. At the end of August he returned to Bad Gastein for two more weeks, arriving back in Vienna on 15 September. For the rest of the year his main psychoanalytic work was on his university lectures which he would deliver in the winter semester of 1916 to 1917.

By the beginning of 1917 Freud was becoming more and more pessimistic about the outcome of the war. Even Germany's U-boat offensive, launched on 1 February, could not inspire hope in him, and the Russian Revolution which occurred later in the same month merited only a brief note in the family calendar. He wrote to Ferenczi that he might have given it more attention if his first concern had not been for peace. With the entry of America into the war in April it seemed that the likelihood of victory for the Central Powers was even more remote. And everyday life in Vienna had become hard, with fuel and food scarce, prices exorbitant and much only available on the black market. Freud would have been greatly surprised to have been awarded the Nobel Prize, but his brief entry, 'No Nobel Prize 1917' in the calendar on 25 April, does reveal some disappointment. As a sign of international recognition it would have been welcome, and he needed the money. At the start of the year Freud did not have any patients, though by April he had a few. His regular income was therefore proving to be inadequate.

During the summer of that year it was impossible to obtain accommodation in the countryside of Austria, either in Bad Gastein or on the Semmering Pass. Eventually Ferenczi solved the problem for the family by finding a pleasant place high up in the Tatra Mountains, in Slovakia, called Csorbató. It turned out to be quite cold with frequent stormy weather, but they stayed there for two months, with Freud able to indulge in his hobby of collecting mushrooms. There were frequent visitors, including Rank, Eitingon, Sachs and Ferenczi. The family travelled back to Vienna via Budapest, arriving there on 31 August. During the return journey he wrote a short paper about Goethe entitled 'A Childhood Recollection from *Dichtung und Wahrheit*'. In the autumn his practice improved, and he had nine patients during the rest of the year.

With the continuing food and fuel shortages in Vienna during the winter of 1917–18 Freud was grateful indeed for the efforts of Karl von Freund and Ferenczi to get some supplies of extra food through to them whenever they could, even though it meant abusing their military positions. Then in February there was a very welcome surprise: a patient who had been very satisfied with Freud's treatment left him 10,000 Kronen in his will. This was not a particularly enormous sum given the economic situation of the time, but it did enable Freud to be more generous to members of his family than he had been able to be for some time. Generally his mood was not very cheerful at this time, however, especially as he had long held the completely irrational conviction that he would die in February 1918. This caused him additional anguish at the thought he might die before his mother, who would be eighty-three that year and suffer greatly if he pre-deceased her.

During the summer of 1918 an event occurred which greatly boosted Freud's morale. Another grateful patient, a Hungarian, Dr Anton von Freund, whom Freud had successfully treated for a neurosis which had developed as a result of anxiety about the recurrence of testicular cancer, decided to devote his considerable wealth to supporting the cause of psychoanalysis. Primarily he financed a publishing house, which would enable the movement to be completely independent of other publishers. This became known generally as the *Verlag*, the common term for 'publishing house' in German.

Another event which raised the spirits of psychoanalysts in general was the successful arrangement of a conference, to be held at the end of the summer period, towards the end of September. Before that came the usual family holidays, which, with Ferenczi's help again, were at the same location as the previous year in the Tatra Mountains. Freud first travelled by ship with his daughter Anna to Steinbruch in Hungary. His wife had gone to Schwerin to visit their second daughter, Sophie. The Freuds stayed in Csorbató until the end of August and then moved for a while to a villa in Lomnicz, not far away. At the end of September Freud went to Budapest, where the Fifth International Psychoanalytical Congress was held on 28–29 September. It was the first conference at which members of national governments were present, for one topic on the agenda was to be war neuroses. Abraham and Ferenczi, amongst others, had published research on the topic which had impressed some high-ranking officers. Generally the atmosphere at the conference was buoyant and optimistic and Freud now considered

Budapest to be the centre of the psychoanalytic movement. This was reinforced by the election of Ferenczi as President of the International Association. Those critics of psychoanalysis who declare it an elitist cure for the well-heeled would do well to consider Freud's own lecture on that occasion in which he advocated the establishment of psychoanalytic clinics for the poor.

In the course of September there was steady progress towards the establishment of a final peace in Europe, and by the end of the month the Central Powers were ready to negotiate a treaty. But while there was general relief at the cessation of hostilities, there were also hard times ahead. Basic provisions continued to be scarce, and Freud found himself at the onset of autumn with no patients. His views on the international political situation had changed greatly in the course of the war and on 25 October he was able to write to Ferenczi: 'I shall not weep a single tear for the fate of Austria or Germany.'[10] With the collapse of the Hapsburg Empire chaos ensued and, as elsewhere in Europe, a state of revolution arose. Though violence did occur, protests in Austria were generally much more seemly affairs, such that Hanns Sachs imagined, in a much-quoted letter to Ernest Jones, that placards would soon be held aloft proclaiming: 'The Revolution will take place tomorrow at two-thirty; in the case of unfavourable weather it will be held indoors.'[11] However there were battles with live ammunition on the streets between radical groups and those concerned to preserve the old order, and Freud had to run for cover on one occasion when he was taking a walk with his daughter Mathilde. Many of his colleagues were so anxious about the situation that they urged Freud to move to another country: Ferenczi was keen for him to go to Hungary, Sachs and Pfister supported the move to Switzerland, and Jones assured him of a welcome in England. Despite his continuing dislike of Vienna, however, Sigmund decided to stay there. One reason might well have been a reluctance to move very far afield while there was still no news of the whereabouts of his eldest son Martin. There was a rumour that he had been captured by the Italians, and it was not until December that news arrived of his presence in an Italian hospital near Genoa. He would be finally released before August of the following year.

The New Year, 1919, saw little improvement in the general circumstances of the Freuds, and Sigmund's correspondence throughout the early spring reveals his concerns about the health of his family and the general shortage of food and other provisions. The hardships afflicted all Viennese at the time: beef was only supplied to people working in essential services and milk was extremely scarce. Fuel for heating was also hard to come by. But at least Freud now had some patients again: in January he had reported that he was treating nine or ten patients every day. In May his wife Martha suffered from a severe attack of influenza, and though Freud was advised that it was not a particularly dangerous strain, they were all lacking in sufficient nourishment to fight it; many thousands had died of it in the preceding winter. Martha needed a long period of recuperation and it was not until July that she regained her health fully.

It was in July too that a death occurred in Freud's immediate circle of colleagues, which however did not move him in any deep way. Victor Tausk had originally studied journalism and law, but had become interested in psychoanalysis and proved himself to be a good analyst and an impressive lecturer. His experiences during the war had however caused him severe mental strain. His relationships with women were volatile. There had been early signs of this in his brief fling with Lou Andreas-Salomé. Since then he had been married, divorced, and engaged again several times. He had asked Freud to take him into analysis, but, although Freud had helped him financially in the past, he now refused to help him, and sent him instead to Helene Deutsch who was herself in analysis with Freud. This naturally led to each member of the triangle talking to one of the others about the third, clearly a rather precarious arrangement. Shortly before he was due to get married again, Tausk succumbed to a severe fit of depression and somehow contrived to shoot and hang himself at the same time. Freud was not alone in feeling that his death was no great loss to psychoanalysis. Lou Andreas-Salomé admitted that she had long sensed that Tausk's presence had been detrimental to the cause of psychoanalysis. Tausk's fate did however contribute to Freud's growing interest in a psychoanalytic understanding of death.

With his wife still weak from her illness, it was decided that she should spend a month in the summer at a sanatorium. Freud himself went with Minna to one of his favourite Austrian spas, Bad Gastein. It was something of a self-indulgence, given his financial hardship, but he felt it was justified by the need to restore his energy for the winter ahead.

In the meantime conditions had not improved in Vienna. In October he wrote to his nephew Samuel, now a prosperous businessman in Manchester, England, explaining just how dire things were. Most people who could consider themselves middle-class had lost virtually all their wealth and were near destitution; foreign imports had dried up; and the lack of fuel and raw materials had brought most industry to a standstill. Freud's brother-in-law, now living in America, had been able to help them out financially to some extent, and this enabled Freud to pay for his mother and sisters Dolfi and Pauli to spend the winter at the spa town of Ischl, to avoid the inevitable hardships of the coming months. Max Eitingon in Berlin also sent him some money, and, something which was especially important to enable him to work, a supply of cigars.

It should also be recorded at this juncture that in October 1919 Freud was finally appointed a full professor of the University of Vienna, but it was a rather empty honour as he was not also a member of the Board of the Faculty. The appointment carried with it no obligation to lecture, so that students were not obliged to attend those lectures which he organised privately.

In these circumstances Freud became increasingly dependent on foreign patients, which meant that most of his analytical sessions had to be conducted in English. This made him aware of the inadequacy of his own command of the language and during that autumn he employed a private tutor to help him improve his ability. He also worked at this time with an English doctor, David Forsyth, who rather spoiled Freud with his clear English diction; it made it more difficult for him to cope with the unfamiliar accents of his regular patients. He persisted with the lessons, however, for several years.

In late January 1920, there occurred another death which moved Freud far more deeply than that of Tausk. His benefactor and founder of the *Verlag*, Dr Anton von Freund, suffered a recurrence of his cancer and died at the age of forty. He had become a close friend and Freud visited him daily during his final illness. His decline took several months, so that Freud could gradually accustom himself to the inevitable, but then, only five days after the death of von Freund there occurred another death which shocked Freud greatly: his daughter Sophie, pregnant with her third child, died suddenly of the influenza, complicated by pneumonia, which had affected so many of late. She was only twenty-six years old. Due to the problems with the transport system at the time it was not possible to travel to Hamburg to provide some comfort to Sophie's husband, who was left with one son of six years and another of only thirteen months. Freud and his wife never really overcame the loss, and he would refer to it on many occasions in the future when comforting friends on their bereavements. Not being a man who could turn to religion for consolation Freud could only plunge himself into his work. The immediate products of those first few years after the end of the war were some studies on homosexuality, a paper on the topic of telepathy, which had long intrigued him, and the work known in English as *Beyond the Pleasure Principle*, published in 1920. The fact that this work features centrally the concept of a 'death drive' ('*Todestrieb*') owes more however to the experiences of the First World War than to Freud's recent personal losses, as it was written mainly in 1919. When others attempted to draw connections with his personal life, Freud emphasised that he had shown an almost completed manuscript of the work to friends in Berlin as early as September 1919. It is an important work, in which Freud visualises the dynamic structure of the mind in a new way, while retaining his older model essentially intact. There are, he argued, forces in the mind which work against the predominance of the pleasure principle. As well as the reality principle, the recognition that fulfilment of pleasure must often be postponed for reasons of practicality or morality, there was also a need in every organism to die in its own way. There was an eternal conflict in the mind between Eros, the procreative force, and Thanatos, the death drive. The exposition is complex and, as Freud himself admitted, goes beyond psychoanalysis into the realms of philosophy. In the context of the present biographical study it is evidence of how extensive the experiences of war, war neuroses and the aftermath were upon Freud's thinking.

Restoring his energy again in Bad Gastein in August 1920, Freud managed, after a period of some respite from intellectual pursuits, to turn his attention to the subject of crowd psychology and the nature of the ego. This work was to be published under the title *Massenpsychologie und Ich-Analyse* (*Group Psychology and the Analysis of the Ego*). His first draft of the book was ready by October. Essentially Freud was changing his focus from the psychology of the individual to that of society in general. There are clear links to many of the conclusions of the earlier work *Totem and Taboo*. Though there would appear to be a change of focus, Freud indicates close links between individual and social psychology, and stresses also that the Other (as an ideal, as an object of interest, and as a figure of authority) had in any case always been perceived by psychoanalysis as playing an important role in the psychology of the individual. Psychoanalysis had always explained the inner world by reference to experience of the outer world. In 1922 Ferenczi published an appreciative review of the work in which he also identified some changes in Freud's usage of terminology, which would be developed in subsequent works.

After staying in Bad Gastein for about a month, Freud went with his daughter Anna to visit Sophie's grieving husband in Hamburg. From here they travelled with Eitingon to the congress which had been arranged at The Hague in early September. After the congress Freud and his daughter had planned a trip to England, but this proved unworkable. Instead two Dutch colleagues took them on a tour of the Netherlands. Freud was at that time already familiar with the main cities from previous visits, and they managed on this occasion to explore some lesser known areas. An unusual highlight was a trip by canoe on some of the waterways of Zeeland. At the end of their trip Anna went back to Hamburg for some time, while Sigmund returned to Vienna via Berlin.

Freud's next major work was realised with clear awareness of the ideas of a maverick among psychoanalysts, Georg Groddeck, though Freud's own ideas differed from his considerably. As head of a sanatorium in Baden-Baden, Groddeck had been freely using psychoanalytical ideas and terminology since early in the new century. Initially he had been sceptical about the basic Freudian tenets but became converted after reading Freud's books on dream analysis and the psychopathology of everyday human behaviour. Despite Groddeck's tendency to be provocative and to indulge in wild speculation, Freud was overcome by his charm. Early in 1921 Groddeck amazed and disturbed many analysts by bringing out what he termed a 'psychoanalytic novel' entitled *The Seeker of Souls*, which was published by the *Verlag*. While many other psychoanalysts decried the work, Freud appreciated Groddeck's sense of humour and compared him with Rabelais. In the spring of 1921 Groddeck began to send some chapters of a new book for Freud's consideration. They were written in the form of letters to an imaginary woman friend, and Freud admitted to finding them charming. In the chapters Groddeck developed further a concept of 'It' ('Es') which he had formulated some years before, and which was intended to incorporate something more extensive in scope than the psychoanalytical unconscious. Freud had been developing similar ideas independent of Groddeck for some time, at least since 1917. As it happens Freud used the same German word 'Es' in his own theory, but this has acquired the standardised translation in English of 'Id' (from the Latin rendering in the standard edition of his works). Groddeck's book *The Book of the It* was eventually published early in 1923 and Freud's book, known commonly as *The Ego and the Id*, was published only a few weeks later. Groddeck felt that Freud had usurped his own ideas, but Freud, recognising the stimulus that Groddeck had provided him, argued that his 'Id' did not have the overpowering force which Groddeck attributed to his 'It'. Freud granted the 'Ego' much more influence in the conduct of human affairs than Groddeck was willing to admit.

Freud continued working hard with analyses and with his writing in the first half of 1922, and was as ever determined to ensure himself and his family a long summer vacation. His growing fame meant that many patients started to seek treatment from him during these precious months of relaxation, but Freud generally remained firm, even though it often meant a considerable loss of income. Thus in the summer of 1922, while staying in Berchtesgaden, he refused to see either a woman whose husband was a rich copper magnate, or a wealthy American woman for whom money seemed to be no object.

Although Freud seemed to be healthy and was maintaining a heavy workload he did admit to Ernest Jones in June 1922 that he was feeling tired, especially at the effects of the political conflicts dominating Viennese life at that time. In July he reported feeling much better after escaping to Bad Gastein again. But by August he wrote to Rank from Berchtesgaden that in fact he was feeling far from well and asked him not to reveal this fact to others. In the middle of August, however, occurred an event which took his mind off his own condition: his niece, Cäcilie Graf, only twenty-three years old and pregnant but unmarried, committed suicide by taking an overdose of veronal. In the note she left behind she reassured her lover that it was not his fault.

Towards the end of his summer vacation Freud went back to Hamburg to see his son-in-law and grandchildren again before going on to the congress, which that year was held in Berlin. Jones recorded that there were 256 people in attendance and that over the previous two years the international membership had risen from 191 to 239. It turned out to be the last international conference that Freud himself would be able to attend.

There were two other events of particular interest in the latter part of 1922. The first was remarkable indeed: in November, the son of one of Freud's servants shot his father on discovering him raping his half-sister. Fortunately the father survived. Freud was so concerned about the possible fate of the disturbed young man that he paid all the legal expenses for the young man's defence himself. The second significant event was the arrival in the world of someone who has since become internationally famous in his own right as an artist: on 8 December Ernst and his wife provided Freud with his fifth grandson, Lucian Freud.

By the middle of February 1923, Freud had become aware of a growth on his jaw and palate. It was diagnosed as a benign growth known as leukoplakia associated with heavy smoking. Out of fear that his doctor might order him to stop smoking Freud kept the fact secret from everyone for some time.

Living with 'The Monster' and the Crisis with Rank (1923–8)

By April 1923, a growth on Freud's jaw and palate, which had first started to cause him some discomfort late in 1917, and which had been diagnosed as benign by his doctor, had become too large to ignore any longer. A dermatologist, Maximilian Steiner, reassured Freud and told him that it was nothing to worry about, and that he should just give up smoking. But a doctor whom Freud trusted, Felix Deutsch, examined him on 7 April and, though he realised that the growth was cancerous, he told Freud it was a bad leukoplakia which could easily be removed. Freud agreed to undergo the recommended surgery but chose a doctor, Marcus Hajek, to perform it, even though he had little trust in his competence. There was a mishap on the operating table and Freud suffered heavy bleeding both during and after the operation. As no other room was available at that time he was taken to lie down in a small room which he had to share with a mentally handicapped dwarf. Martha and Anna, who had come to the hospital with a few of his personal things, were reassured by the staff and encouraged to go home. But when they returned in the afternoon they learned that Sigmund had suffered a sudden attack of profuse bleeding. He had tried to get help but the alarm bell was out of order and due to the after-effects of the operation he could not attract attention. It was the dwarf who saved him. Realising his roommate's plight he rushed out in search of a nurse. Shocked by the clinic's neglect of its important patient Anna refused to move from his side and spent the night sitting on a chair in the company of her father and the dwarf. During the night Freud suffered excruciating pain but the house surgeon refused to come to his aid. By late the following day he was allowed to go home.

To family and friends Freud put on a cheerful face and played down the seriousness of his condition, which he was probably aware of even though the details were kept from him. At about the same time, Sophie's younger son, Heinerle, had his tonsils removed, and during a stay in Vienna with his Aunt Matthilde, he and Freud discussed together their difficulties in eating. Freud was very fond of the boy, who had developed a tubercular condition in the previous year. On 19 June he died at the age of four and a half. Freud was devastated at the loss and it was reported that he dissolved into tears. It distressed him more profoundly than any other death he had had to endure, and certainly more than his own cancerous condition; he developed severe depression, which deprived him of all ability to find enjoyment in life.

In the next few months Freud had several further consultations with Dr Hajek, who consented to him going on his usual summer holiday on the condition that he send fortnightly reports of his condition. Even though a local doctor in Bad Gastein reassured him about his condition, Freud asked Felix Deutsch to come and examine him while he and the family were in Lavarone. Deutsch realised that further operations would be necessary, but he did not reveal the full extent of Freud's condition to him, partly because of Freud's depressed state of mind.

Already on the occasion of his first operation in April, with undeniable intimations of mortality, Freud had decided to fulfil without delay his long-held wish to visit Rome with his daughter Anna. Despite his worsening condition he realised his dream during September and took great delight in his daughter's pleasure in everything he showed her in the city. By the end of the month he faced the need to undergo two further operations, involving work on the upper jaw. At Deutsch's recommendation they were to be carried out by an eminent oral surgeon on 4 and 12 October. As a result Freud was unable to eat or speak for some time. Later in the month some further cancerous tissue had to be removed, and in the coming years there would have to be thirty or so further operations to keep the cancer in check. In addition he had to wear a prosthesis constantly, the function of which was to block the gap between the mouth and the nasal cavity. This proved to be very uncomfortable and difficult to remove and replace, and Freud came to refer to it as 'the monster'. Side effects were a lack of facility in speech and, due to local infection, a loss of hearing in the right ear. Naturally enough his medical problems made it impossible for him to see any patients during the rest of the year, with the result that while his medical expenses were increasing his income declined.

By the beginning of January 1924, Freud was again able to see six patients on a regular basis, even though he found the work very tiring. In February a second prosthesis had to be made and fitted, but it was as much bother as the first. The spring did bring some cheer with the birth of a third son to Ernst and his wife on 24 April, and there was the prospect of yet more grandchildren on the way: both Oliver's and Martin's wives were pregnant. On Freud's sixty-eighth birthday in May the city council of Vienna, realising that one of their famous citizens might not be much longer for this world, decided to bring forward an award usually made on a person's seventieth birthday, and granted him 'Freedom of the City' (*'Bürgerrecht'*). At about the same time Freud received a curious request. A journalist with the *Chicago Tribune* sent a telegram to Freud asking him virtually to name his price to come and conduct a psychoanalysis of two men, whose names were to become famous, the would-be 'perfect murderers' Leopold and Loeb. Their story was the basis of a successful play which Alfred Hitchcock turned into the film *Rope*. Freud replied to the journalist on 24 June explaining that he felt he was not in a position to offer any expert opinions with such scant knowledge of the case, and certainly could not take up the invitation to go to New York for the period of the trial due to his precarious health.

Throughout 1924 Freud also had to deal with the increasingly erratic and disturbed behaviour of Otto Rank. Freud had greatly supported Rank since their first meeting in 1905, when the young man, who had mostly taught himself, came to see him with the complete manuscript of a book entitled *The Artist*. Freud took a paternal interest in him, helping him in his academic career. He proved to be very useful to Freud, often functioning as a kind of amanuensis, and was the founder and editor of the periodical *Imago*, started in 1912, and then, in 1913, of the *Internationale Zeitschrift*. By 1923, however, Rank was showing frequent signs of mental instability, occasionally, for example, bursting into fits of hysterical laughter. Others around Freud became worried about Rank's condition long before Freud did himself. Even when Rank's ideas began to diverge considerably from his own Freud remained generous towards him. In 1922 Rank wrote a book together with Ferenczi, which was published early in 1924 under the title *The Development of Psychoanalysis*. Rank also published a book called *The Trauma of Birth* which emphasised that the fantasy of returning to the womb was more influential in mental development than the later traumatic experiences which Freud focused on. Still Freud was tolerant of their differences. It was Abraham who first impressed upon Freud the fact that the ideas of Rank and Ferenczi were challenging some of the basic tenets of psychoanalysis. Finally Freud had to admit to some doubt about the effectiveness of the method of shortening the process of analysis which the two colleagues were advocating. For Freud this would involve treating by suggestion rather than through understanding. Freud also came to see that Rank in particular was making the mother's role more important in psychological development and thereby reducing the significance of the Oedipus complex. By late March 1924, Freud was writing to Ferenczi that he now found only about one third of the ideas in Rank's book correct. In April Rank went to America, where he held lectures and seminars, in which he propagated his ideas about methods of shortening the analytical process and the importance of the birth trauma. Freud continued to hope that Rank, who had been so close to him, would remain in the fold.

Freud had planned to spend part of the summer in Switzerland, but the continuing problems with his cancer made it necessary for him to stay near Vienna on the Semmering. Abraham, who had been holidaying in the Engadine, visited Freud for a few days in early August. It was to be the last time that they would meet. During August and September Freud wrote the first draft of his 'Autobiographical Study', which was to be published in the following year.

By the end of the summer vacation period Freud was coming more and more to realise that the criticisms of Rank were sound, even though he still wished to maintain a good personal relationship with him. Jones had been warning him frequently in letters and he now, reluctantly, came to admit that Jones had been right. When Rank came back to Vienna from America it was clear that the experience had gone to his head. He resigned his official posts, and, finding that now even Ferenczi was against him, he planned to go back to America where, presumably, he felt that he was better appreciated. His indecisive state of mind was revealed in his erratic behaviour in November. He went to the station to take a train as the first stage on another trip to America, only to turn up at his home in Vienna again a few hours later. Towards the end of November he set off for America once more and this time got as far as Paris before returning to Vienna yet again. By the middle of December he was in a completely distraught state of mind and having daily consultations with Freud. Finally, on 20 December, he sent a letter to all his colleagues which amounted to a recantation. In the letter he interpreted his severe neurotic condition in conventional Freudian terms and apologised to all profusely. On Christmas Day Abraham, together with other Berlin colleagues, sent a letter to Rank which was both conciliatory and gently reprimanding.

The result, however, was that Rank did eventually pluck up enough resolve to make it all the way to America in January 1925.

Freud felt that the last few months of 1924 and the beginning of 1925 had been a very unproductive period for him, though inspiration had returned to him by the late spring. In the spring also came the first signs of severe ill health in Karl Abraham. After giving some lectures in Holland he developed a persistent bronchial cough. In June came the sad news that Freud's earlier mentor Josef Breuer had died at the age of eighty-four on the 20th. Despite the differences they had had Freud sent sincere condolences to his family and wrote an obituary for him.

During the summer Abraham experienced some improvement in his condition but at the congress held in Homburg from 2–5 September he appeared to his colleagues a very sick man trying to cope with his condition through the use of morphium. During this period Abraham became involved with Freud in a rather bizarre scheme originating in America to embroil Freud in the fantasy world of Hollywood. The producer Samuel Goldwyn offered Freud $100,000 to participate in the making of a film about the great love stories of history. Hanns Sachs, witty as ever, is said to have claimed that Freud's telegram of blunt refusal had caused a greater stir in America than *The Interpretation of Dreams*. It was agreed in June that the film would be made with the collaboration of the famous German film company Ufa and that it would, under the guidance of a respected psychoanalyst, demonstrate some of the principles of psychoanalysis. Abraham expressed the opinion that, if it was to be made at all, it would be better to ensure that it would be in the hands of someone who knew what he was talking about. Freud did not object but he refused to have anything to do with it. Much to his annoyance the film company announced in August that the film, *The Mystery of the Soul*, was being made 'with Freud's cooperation'. The whole matter created bad feeling between Freud and Abraham, with the latter believing that Freud was not showing sufficient respect for his judgement.

Freud remained concerned, however, about the continuing deterioration in Abraham's health. By October Abraham was suffering from a painfully swollen liver. Abraham had sought Fliess's advice on his condition and this led to the first personal contact between Freud and Fliess after their separation of twenty years. It has been subsequently ascertained that Abraham must have been suffering from lung cancer. By the middle of December it became clear that Abraham would not survive much longer, and on Christmas Day he died at the age of forty-eight. Freud was greatly shocked at the loss, feeling that Abraham had been one of his staunchest supporters.

Early in the New Year, in the middle of February 1926, Freud suffered some recurrence of problems with his heart. At first he was reluctant to let the matter disturb his daily rhythm, putting it down to an excessive intake of tobacco, but finally he agreed to take the advice of a doctor friend and spent several weeks in a sanatorium, which he entered on 5 March. Here, nursed alternately by his wife, Anna and Minna, he continued to conduct sessions with three patients. Freud felt that since his heart condition had forced him to give up smoking, he was experiencing a reduction in his intellectual powers. His main worry was that, if his health continued to be poor, he would not be able to earn enough money to support his preferred lifestyle and those who were dependent on him. He finally returned to the Berggasse on 2 April.

It was also in April that Rank visited Freud for the last time. It is clear that during his period in the sanatorium Freud had reconciled himself to the final break.

The crisis with Rank contributed greatly to the next major work, which was to appear during 1926: *Inhibitions, Symptoms and Anxiety*. In this work Freud dealt directly with the challenges presented by Rank's ideas, especially those on the trauma of birth. The other significant work published in 1926 was also in direct response to an issue concerning a colleague, but this time Freud was vehemently defending the younger man. The issue dated back several years. In the latter part of 1924 Freud had been asked to provide his expert opinion on the matter of permitting psychoanalysis to be conducted by laymen, what has become known as lay analysis. Freud was enthusiastic about the opportunity to defend his standpoint in favour of such analysis. But early in 1925 Theodor Reik was accused by the city authorities of practising medicine without due qualifications. It led to a complex legal case, during which Reik was ordered to cease practising. With Freud's support he managed successfully to appeal the decision. But in the spring of 1926 an American patient whom Freud had passed on to Reik sued the latter on a charge of medical malpractice. Freud promptly wrote a spirited defence under the title *The Question of Lay Analysis*. To friends he declared that he would never give up the fight to maintain the right of psychoanalysis to train its own adherents. He would never contemplate its inclusion as a branch of medicine. Eventually the charges against Reik were dropped, though the debate about lay analysis was to continue for several years.

Freud was very much aware that it would prove extremely difficult to avoid considerable public attention on the occasion of his seventieth birthday in May. He toyed with the idea of escaping attention completely by shutting himself off in the sanatorium again for a week or so. He used his heart condition as an excuse to refuse many invitations, such as that to participate in a special festive edition of a leading Viennese medical journal. This could not prevent all the major Viennese newspapers from publishing special articles to mark the occasion, including one by Stefan Zweig, but the various academic societies of Vienna University deliberately snubbed Freud by ignoring the event. A Jewish lodge, the B'nai B'rith, of which Freud was a member, published a volume of appreciative essays. But most pleasing to Freud were personal letters of congratulation from Einstein, Romain Rolland and Yvette Guilbert, whom he had first seen perform during his time in Paris, and whose annual concerts in Vienna he never missed. On the actual day, 6 May, Freud was visited by ten of his followers who presented him with a collection (equivalent to over $4,000) drawn from members of the Psychoanalytic Association. Freud donated most of it to the *Verlag* and the rest to the Psychoanalytic Clinic.

From June to September Freud stayed on the Semmering again, in the Villa Schüler. He had to agree to regular trips back to Vienna during this time to undergo adjustments to the prosthesis, and his heart condition was still giving some cause for concern. Ferenczi spent a week with him towards the end of August before going on a trip to America in September.

On returning to Vienna for the autumn Freud decided to reduce his number of patients from six to five, but raised his fees to cover the loss in income. Since he felt unable to conduct regular meetings, he now arranged for a select group of colleagues to visit him on the second Friday of every month for discussion. Positive developments that autumn were the opening of the London Clinic of Psychoanalysis in September, and evidence of the growing global interest in psychoanalysis, demonstrated by the visit of a psychiatrist from Rio de Janeiro who presented Freud with a book containing forty pages devoted to the subject. On 25 October Freud also agreed to meet the famous Indian author Rabindranath Tagore, who was on a visit to Vienna, and in November Ernst Simmel opened a psychoanalytic clinic to treat alcohol addiction near the Tegelsee, Berlin. In December Freud, together with his wife, undertook his first extensive journey since his operation three years previously. They travelled to Berlin with the main intent of seeing their two sons and four grandchildren. It was also the occasion of a meeting with Albert Einstein, who visited the Freuds in the company of his own wife. Freud wrote to Ferenczi of the meeting: 'He understands as much about psychology as I do about physics, so we had a very pleasant talk.'[12]

Ferenczi was received very warmly in America and gave talks to various institutions. He also undertook the training of a number of people as lay analysts, but this brought him into conflict with leading psychoanalysts in New York, who, on 25 January 1927, passed a resolution condemning lay analysis. This led to growing tension between him and even the most well-wishing of his American colleagues.

One of the main concerns of the Viennese psychoanalysts in the spring of that year was the desperate financial situation of the *Verlag*. It finally came to serious negotiations with a commercial firm to try and sell the stock. Freud was most reluctant to lose control of the company, fearing that if that happened they would never be able to regain it. Disaster was finally staved off by a large donation from a grateful benefactress.

Doctors familiar with Freud's health noticed some general decline compared with the previous year and recommended a further stay in the sanatorium. Freud was as ever reluctant at first but was finally persuaded to spend a week there in April. He subsequently reduced his number of patients from five to three. In June Freud wrote a short supplement to his essay on Michelangelo's statue of Moses. The supplement was published first in a French language psychoanalytic periodical and in *Imago* at the end of the year. From 16 June till the end of September the family stayed again at the Villa Schüler on the Semmering, but during August Freud complained of frequent weakness and discomfort. There was some bad feeling in the relationship between Freud and Ernest Jones in September, due to Jones having written an article which revealed some sympathy for Melanie Klein's theories about child analysis. Freud suspected Jones of implying criticism of his daughter Anna's views. The matter was settled calmly, though Freud remained sceptical of Klein's methods.

Apart from papers on fetishism and humour the most well-known work of Freud's written during 1927 was his critical analysis of religion, *The Future of an Illusion*. He had started writing it in the spring and the proofs were ready by late October. Freud was disparaging of the book's worth but it does outline very clearly his views on the nature, in psychoanalytic terms, of religion. He had been planning such a work for a long time but had held back out of fear of offending his good friend Oskar Pfister. When he wrote to Pfister about it, the latter was as magnanimous as ever, replying that he would rather read the opinions of an intelligent unbeliever like Freud than the words of a thousand unintelligent believers.

In the course of 1927 Groddeck had been lobbying to have Freud's name proposed for the Nobel Prize, and in February 1928 Jones reports that further efforts were being undertaken. When he heard of it, however, Freud was irritated and dismissive of the whole plan. At about the same time he suffered from severe conjunctivitis in one eye which made reading extremely difficult for about six weeks. Apart from this infliction, he was still suffering considerable pain and discomfort from the condition of his jaw, and not unnaturally he was feeling generally very tired. In April he suffered the loss of another old friend, Ludwig Rosenberg, one of the three with whom he played his weekly game of cards. Through the agency of his son, Ernst, a famous oral surgeon, a Professor Schroeder, came from Berlin to examine Freud late in June. Freud was encouraged by the way the surgeon examined him that he agreed to travel to Berlin to undergo treatment. He kept the plan quiet so as not to offend his Viennese physicians, and, under the pretence that the main purpose of the trip was to visit his offspring, he left Vienna for Berlin on 30 August to stay at the sanatorium at Tegel. Although he suffered considerable discomfort during his stay and could barely talk, he was cheered by visits from friends, especially Ferenczi and Marie Bonaparte. When he returned to Vienna at the beginning of November, he was wearing a new prosthesis which was much more comfortable than the old one.

In December news came of the death of Wilhelm Fliess. His wife wrote to Freud asking him to send her the letters which Fliess had written to Freud. But, after a thorough search, he had to report that he had destroyed them. This prompted him to remind Frau Fliess that he would not like his own letters to her husband to fall into unscrupulous hands.

While several of his works were published for the first time in 1928, the generally poor condition of Freud's health meant that he was unable to work extensively on any new projects. A notable contribution to the psychoanalysis of literary figures, which he had started in 1926, but put aside to dash off his polemical work on lay analysis, finally appeared in this year. This was the extensive essay entitled *Dostoyevsky and Parricide*. This had come about as the result of an invitation to write a psychoanalytical introduction to an academic study of Dostoyevsky's *The Brothers Karamazov*. The essay had been finished some time early in 1927.

During the winter of 1928–9 the *Verlag* was undergoing another of its serious financial crises, but fortunately it was saved by several generous donations, the first being in January by Princess Marie Bonaparte, a great-granddaughter of Lucien Napoleon, the Emperor's brother. She was a wealthy and prominent person, highly intelligent and unconventional in her views and tastes. After undergoing some analysis with Freud she became an enthusiastic advocate of psychoanalysis and a close friend of Freud's. By March other donations arrived, including one from a patient who wished to remain anonymous. On 11 March, Freud went with Anna to Berlin again for a fortnight to have further consultations with Professor Schroeder. As before they stayed near the Tegelsee. At about this time Marie Bonaparte also recommended that Freud take on Dr Max Schur as a regular personal physician to ensure that his health was being constantly checked. Freud readily agreed and the two men became firm friends. Apart from a few short periods Schur remained close to Freud for the rest of his life, and Freud made Schur promise him two things: to always tell him the truth about his condition, and not to let him suffer pain unnecessarily.

Honours, and Problems with Ferenczi
(1929–33)

After managing to keep his birthday visitors to a minimum in May 1929 (Eitingon and Lou Andreas-Salomé being the only ones), Freud set off on 18 June to spend the summer at Schneewinkel, near Berchtesgaden. Having had to spend many summers on the Semmering close to Vienna for the sake of his health, Freud was pleased to be in one of his favourite scenic areas again. He received a considerable number of visitors there over the next few months, including Jones and Ferenczi. Towards the end of the holiday, it did become necessary, however, to spend several weeks in Berlin again for treatment.

In the course of 1929 the relationship between Freud and Ferenczi was clearly deteriorating. Jones's account of this may well have been coloured by the fact that Ferenczi had been conveying hostile views of him to Freud. According to Jones Ferenczi had been disappointed not to be made President of the International Association at the congress in Oxford at the end of July. At this congress he also developed some ideas which were at odds with Freud's current views on the aetiology of neuroses. Ferenczi's visit to Freud during the summer was followed by a long silence. He later explained to Freud that his silence had been out of fear that Freud would not agree with his new ideas.

Starting that July, Freud was also working on a new book. This was to be his extensive application of psychoanalytic theory to understanding the nature of civilised society, *Das Unbehagen in der Kultur*. The standard rendering has become *Civilisation and its Discontents*. It proved to be a bestseller, with the first edition of 12,000 being sold out within a year, but Freud was never really satisfied with the work.

In the first few months of 1930 Ferenczi continued to feel extremely sensitive about his relationship with Freud. Freud wrote to him very sympathetically about his being passed over as President of the International Association, but expressed his inability to understand why Ferenczi should feel hostile towards him. By the time Ferenczi came to visit Freud on 21 April many of his friend's anxieties had been allayed, and the men managed to get back onto an amicable footing again, though Ferenczi continued to suffer from extreme sensitiveness. Shortly after Ferenczi's visit Freud had to spend some time in the sanatorium again due to his cardiac problems and other ailments. Then on 4 May he went to Berlin again to have a new prosthesis made, staying as usual near Tegelsee. For a while he could not bear smoking cigars, but after three weeks or so he was soon back on the old habit again. He had planned to stay in Berlin for no more than six weeks, but it became necessary in the end for him to stay there for more than twelve weeks altogether. There was a pleasant three-day escape towards the end of May, when he was able to visit a small fisherman's cottage which his son Ernst had bought on the island of Hiddensee, near Rügen. This was also the occasion of the only flight in an airplane which Freud made in his life.

It was also during this stay in Berlin that Freud became involved with the American Ambassador, W.C. Bullitt, in writing a psychoanalytic study of President Woodrow Wilson. Freud had long had some interest in Wilson, having hoped he would prove to be something of a saviour in the mire of international politics, but during the period of the peace negotiations at Versailles after the First World War he had lost his faith in him, finding that he had promised far more than he could ever deliver. For some time Freud was reluctant to become involved with

Bullitt's project, believing that psychoanalysis should never be used for political purposes and feeling that his strong dislike of Wilson would prejudice his judgement. Many critics believe that Freud should have heeded his first misgivings and never committed himself to work on the book. The book as it finally appeared after Freud's death was an uneasy mixture of Freud's ideas and Bullitt's belligerent style. It seems likely that Bullitt rewrote much of it after Freud's death, and only the introduction can be attributed with certainty to Freud as it bears his name. A detailed analysis of Freud's involvement in the project is provided in Peter Gay's biography.[13] One strong motivation for Freud's participation seems to have been concern, yet again, for the financial plight of the *Verlag*. It was likely that sales of the book on Wilson would greatly boost the income of the company.

In July, Freud and his family set off for what would prove to be his last holiday away from Vienna, at Rebenburg on the Grundlsee, in the Salzkammergut. Just after they arrived on 28 July he received a letter announcing that he had been awarded the Goethe Prize for excellence in style in scientific writing. It was awarded by the city of Frankfurt and the citation compared Freud to Goethe's Faust in his insatiable pursuit of knowledge and truth. Another notable figure who had received the prize was Albert Schweitzer. Freud's daughter attended the ceremony on his behalf, which took place in Frankfurt on Goethe's birthday, 28 August. Especially pleasing for Freud was the sum of 10,000 marks which accompanied the award. It was not actually an enormous sum but it helped to cover his medical expenses in Berlin and he used some of it to give gifts. In particular he sent the sum of 1,000 marks to Lou Andreas-Salomé, who was now in her late sixties, in poor health and not especially well off.

In September came the sad news that Sigmund's mother had died at the age of ninety-five. He had last seen her in Vienna at the end of August. His feelings were mixed. He was only too aware that it must affect him at deep unconscious levels, but superficially he had to admit, in correspondence with Jones, that he felt some relief that he had outlived her. He had always dreaded that she would outlive him and so suffer severely from his own death. He felt no great suffering at the loss, and, due to his own ill health and dislike of such occasions he decided not to attend the funeral.

At the end of September Freud was back in Vienna. On 10 October he had to undergo another operation for his cancer. This time it was conducted locally in Vienna. On the 17th he was laid low in bed for ten days with broncho-pneumonia, but by 1 November he was back at work with four patients. Then later in the same month Ferenczi came to visit him and both men were pleased to find that their ideas were not so incompatible as they had feared. Jones reports that he met Eitingon in Paris on 14 December and that they agreed that Ferenczi would be nominated to succeed Eitingon as next President of the International Association. By the last days of 1930 Freud's health appeared to be improving, such that he was allowing himself three or four cigars every day.

In January 1931, Freud was invited by the University of London to deliver the annual Huxley Lecture. The honour had fallen to many other great men in the past, including the surgeon Joseph Lister, the Russian psychologist I.P. Pavlov, and the German pathologist and anthropologist Rudolf Virchow. Freud was a great admirer of T.H. Huxley and sincerely regretted that he was not fit enough to take up the offer. Indeed, his health deteriorated during the next few months and in late April he had to undergo another operation, which exhausted him even more. He was not able to leave the hospital until the day before his seventy-fifth birthday.

On this occasion Freud was unable to stave off considerable international attention. He was overwhelmed with congratulatory letters and telegrams from admirers, known and unknown, from all over the world and bouquets of flowers arrived continuously. In New York a celebratory banquet was held in his honour at the Ritz-Carlton Hotel. This time even Viennese psychiatric institutions sent their congratulations. Apart from his family members Freud refused to see anyone on the birthday itself, with the exception of one friend and a colleague with whom his relationship was going through a sensitive stage: Ferenczi.

On 1 June Freud was able to get away for a summer break, but he could not go far as it was necessary for him to undergo daily medical checks. He stayed in the pleasant Viennese suburb of Pötzleinsdorf. During this summer the first meeting took place between him and the English author H.G. Wells, who had long been an admirer.

It was at about this time that the global economic crisis, which had been initiated with the collapse of the New York stock exchange in October 1929, ushering in the Great Depression, came to impinge seriously on the activities of the psychoanalytic movement worldwide. Many people simply could not afford to undertake psychoanalytic treatment, and the analysts themselves found that they could not afford to attend the international congress planned for the autumn of 1931.

In October, however, Freud's spirits were raised by an unexpected honour that came his way. The town council of his birthplace, Freiberg (now Příbor), decided to affix a bronze plaque with his name to the house where he was born. Sigmund's daughter and son, Anna and Martin, and his brother, Alexander, attended the event on his behalf on 25 October, with Anna reading out a letter from her father. The analysts Max Eitingon and Paul Federn also attended.

In the latter part of the year matters came to a head in Freud's relationship with Ferenczi. There had been ominous signs earlier in the year. In May, Ferenczi had sent Freud a paper he planned to read at the conference, which led to more disagreement. During the summer he reported that he was trying various new techniques in analysis. On his way back from a holiday in Capri, Ferenczi spent several days in Vienna, arriving there on

27 October, and discussed with Freud their differences. It seemed that these were resolved, but by early December Ferenczi wrote to Freud that he had not changed any of his opinions. Their fundamental difference was Ferenczi's development of emotional involvement with his patients. He allowed them to regard him as a loving parent, and he also encouraged mutual analysis, allowing his patients access to his own psychological problems. On 13 December Freud wrote a friendly but stern letter to Ferenczi, warning him of the dangers of arousing erotic needs in his patients which could not be fulfilled. Ferenczi attempted in his reply to reassure Freud, hoping that their differences would not disrupt their personal and professional relationship.

At the beginning of 1932 there was a crisis with another analyst who held diverging views. Wilhelm Reich had presented a paper for publication by the *Zeitschrift* on the subject of combining psychoanalytic and Marxist theories. Freud persuaded Reich to accept the inclusion of an editorial statement that psychoanalysis in no way implied a specific political standpoint, but many colleagues did not want the paper published at all. Finally a compromise was reached whereby the paper would be published but followed by another criticising its views. More worrying for Freud was the ever fragile financial state of the *Verlag* itself. In response to a telegram from Freud, Eitingon came to Vienna in the middle of January to discuss matters. It was agreed that Freud's son, Martin, who had been manager for some time, would try to settle matters with the creditors. It was also agreed that it made better economic sense to base their two periodicals in Vienna, instead of incurring extra postal costs by having one based in Berlin. By February, Freud decided that it would be necessary to appeal to the International Psychoanalytic Association to take over the responsibility for the publications in the future. The response to the appeal was encouraging, but it took most of the rest of the year to sort out the finances of the *Verlag* satisfactorily.

In March 1932, Freud was visited by an author greatly admired by the whole family: Thomas Mann. The two men got on very well and there was obviously an easy understanding between them. Also in March, Freud decided to write another series of *Introductory Lectures* which were published at the end of the year, though they were never actually delivered. His main purpose in writing them was to earn more money for the *Verlag*. Another visit which pleased him took place in April. Ludwig Binswanger, whom Freud had visited in Switzerland when Binswanger's health was in a critical state, came to see him with his daughter. Generally the number of Freud's patients was declining but by now, with his poor health, this did not concern him too much. It only motivated him to write more. Accordingly he started his summer holidays early that year, moving to the same house as before in the suburb of Pötzleinsdorf on 14 May. Here he stayed until the middle of September.

Late in August, ten days before the Congress was due to begin, Ferenczi announced that he would not be standing for election as president due to the fact that his views now conflicted with the generally accepted principles of psychoanalysis. Freud fought hard to persuade him to stay within the fold. But after discussing the matter with him in person Freud realised that Ferenczi had now become unsuitable as a candidate, and Eitingon approached Ernest Jones as the most suitable alternative candidate. At the Congress in Wiesbaden there was some concern that the paper which Ferenczi intended to read was unsuitable for the occasion. However the event went off without any unpleasant friction and Ferenczi took part in all the usual business meetings. After the congress, however, he went on holiday to the south of France, partly for the sake of his health, but he became very ill with an anaemic condition and had to return home early. Thereafter his health was in terminal decline. Freud himself had to undergo yet another operation in October and in November he suffered a severe attack of influenza, with a consequent catarrh which plagued him for over a month.

In a letter to Ferenczi in January 1933, Freud was still conciliatory, and when Ferenczi finally replied in March it was to inform him that his anaemic condition was much worse and that he felt he had also suffered some kind of nervous breakdown. He also begged Freud to leave Vienna as soon as possible for his own safety. If this concern might have been considered excessive at the time, the extreme anxiety of a sick and sensitive man, then it must be remembered that the letter was written shortly after the Reichstag fire in Berlin, which provided the excuse for widespread persecution, especially of Jews, by the Nazis.

Nazism and the Flight from Vienna
(1933–9)

When Freud replied, on 2 April 1933, to Ferenczi's letter full of anxiety about his welfare, he did not yet perceive fully the threat posed by the Hitler regime in Germany. He attempted to reassure his friend that it was not at all certain that the Nazis would take over Austria as well, and even if they did it was unlikely that they would employ the same kind of brutality as they had done in Germany. He feared no personal danger.

On 4 May Ferenczi wrote his last letter to Freud on the occasion of the latter's birthday. It was delivered by Ferenczi's wife and caused Freud to be greatly concerned about his friend's mental as well as physical health. In it Ferenczi wrote of how one of his own American patients believed she could influence his condition by communicating with him through telepathy across the Atlantic. It is not clear whether Ferenczi believed in the woman's powers or not. By the end of the month, on 22 May, Ferenczi was dead. Freud seemed strangely resigned to the loss, and in his correspondence reveals a determination, in spite of all, to remain optimistic.

But the political situation was steadily worsening. The Austrian chancellor, Engelbert Dollfuss, had been ruling using emergency powers since the last part of 1932, and from March 1933, he governed without a parliament. In Germany many psychoanalysts were already finding life too dangerous and decided to emigrate. Among these were Erich Fromm and Max

Eitingon. Freud's sons, Ernst and Oliver, also decided it would be wise to leave. Oliver went first to Vienna and Ernst to London. If the Nazis' attitude to the ideas of Freud had been in any doubt before, it was made unambiguous by including his works in the great burning of books on 10 May. Freud could still view it all with irony, unaware as most people of the holocaust that was to come. He told Jones that he thought mankind had made some progress at least: 'In the Middle Ages they would have burnt me; nowadays they are content with burning my books.'[14] He continued to trust in the power of Austrian laws against the persecution of minorities and to believe in the influence of the League of Nations. By the summer he was less optimistic and wrote to his nephew Samuel about the insecure situation of Austria, but reiterated his determination to stay on. He confirmed his determination by continuing with his practice, spending five hours a day analysing patients. But by February 1934 he was writing to Arnold Zweig that he felt that things could not really go on much longer as they were. Circumstances did not change radically for some time, however. The next major crisis was in July 1934, when Chancellor Dollfuss was murdered by Austrian Nazis in an attempt to stage a coup; but the expected invasion by Germany did not materialise, and the state of emergency continued. None of this prevented Freud from continuing with his work, and in the summer he began work on his last major accomplishment: *Moses and Monotheism*. He determined to keep it a secret from most of his colleagues, telling only Arnold Zweig and Eitingon about it. He was uncertain even about exactly what kind of work it was. His intention was to analyse what the Jewish character actually consisted of and how the man Moses had virtually single-handedly created the Jewish identity. In a letter to Lou Andreas-Salomé he had described it as a 'historical novel'.[15] The work suffered many stops and starts. At times he felt the extent of the task he had set himself was too great for him to accomplish, and by November 1934, he was writing to Arnold Zweig that he found himself too critical of his own findings. Yet the theme and the man Moses continued to obsess him and he admitted to Eitingon that it had become a fixation with him.

As ever, even in the worst of times, Freud did not deny himself breaks away from the Berggasse, and in the spring of 1935 he was writing to the American poetess, Hilda Doolittle, a former patient, of the joys of the garden by the house that they were staying in about twelve minutes' drive from the Berggasse. On this occasion too he reported to her that he was still managing to work for five hours every day. He spent most of the summer in Grinzing too, staying there till the middle of October, and he wrote to Hilda again on his return to the Berggasse in November that he was still able to see five patients a day. He also managed to maintain an extensive correspondence with the other analysts who had either long been abroad or who had recently fled. Amongst others, Hanns Sachs was now in Boston and Max Eitingon had gone to Palestine. And there were the occasional visits by admirers and well-wishers, including, on 13 October, the American author Thornton Wilder.

In May 1936, Freud had to face to the prospect of another major birthday celebration, as he had reached the age of eighty. He felt that the general political situation made it inappropriate to arrange celebratory events, and he managed to persuade Jones to abandon his plan to produce a volume of commemorative essays. Freud was undoubtedly pleased, however, to receive a congratulatory address written by Thomas Mann and Stefan Zweig and signed by 191 writers and artists. Mann also wrote a lecture for the occasion, 'Freud and the Future', of which he gave a private reading for the Freud family on 14 June. An even greater honour came his way at the end of the month with his appointment to the British Royal Society of Medicine: he now belonged to the society which had counted Newton and Darwin amongst its members. In July Freud had to undergo two very painful operations which revealed that the cancer was still virulent. The analysts held their congress at Marienbad that year, on 2 August, so that Anna Freud, who attended it, could easily return to her father at short notice should she be needed. After a short stay in Grinzing again, the Freuds celebrated their golden wedding on 13 September in the company of all their children except Oliver. There was a small crisis for Freud at the end of December when he discovered, in a letter from Marie Bonaparte on 30 December, that a bookseller from Berlin had offered to sell her some of Freud's early manuscripts and the letters to Fliess, which Fliess's widow had sold him. Freud was anxious to buy them with the clear intention of having them destroyed. Marie Bonaparte opposed Freud's efforts and defended the preservation of the documents. Finally, in the course of 1937, she bought them but refused to yield to his entreaties, arguing that it was their duty to preserve them for posterity. She had her way and deposited them in the Rothschild Bank in Vienna.

In the early part of 1937 Freud was working on a paper on psychoanalytic technique, 'Analysis Terminable and Interminable', which revealed the conviction that had been growing in him over the years that the claims of psychoanalysis to actually cure patients must remain modest, and it certainly could not guarantee prevention of a recurrence of neurosis. The paper was to appear in June of that year. There were further concerns about the health of others during the year: his sister-in-law, Minna Bernays, at seventy-two was weak and suffering, and in February came the news that Lou Andreas-Salomé had died in Göttingen. On 30 April he moved to Grinzing again but by the end of the month he was in a sanatorium in Auersperg for another operation. Apart from a few other minor health problems the summer that year was comfortable and enjoyable. He also managed to make some further progress with the book on Moses, though after reporting that he had finished a major part of it in August, he announced a few weeks later that he was rewriting another part. By December 1937 Freud could no longer maintain his optimism about the political situation, and he wrote to Arnold Zweig on 20 December that he felt that Austrians seemed to be of the same mind as the German Nazis in their vehement anti-Semitism.

In February 1938, Hitler forced the Austrian chancellor, Kurt von Schuschnigg, to appoint a man he favoured, Seyss-Inquart, as minister of security and the interior. Schuschnigg called a plebiscite for 13 March to gain support for Austrian independence. Freud refused to share in the general sense of panic. He believed that Schusnigg was upright and honest in his promise that Austrian Jews had nothing to fear. He also believed that the Catholic Church would offer strong resistance. But Schuschnigg was finally forced to cancel the plebiscite and on 11 March, following Hitler's ultimatum, he resigned in favour of Seyss-Inquart. On the morning of 12 March the new chancellor invited the German army into Austria. Freud followed events on the radio, realising that this meant indeed the end of Austria, which was, within a week of the invasion renamed the 'Ostmark'.

This is not a suitable context in which to retell the well-known facts of the Nazi takeover of Austria. Suffice it to say that within a matter of weeks Nazi anti-Semitic policies were implemented everywhere, with a thorough purging of all important professional institutions and cultural organisations of their Jewish members. Hitler himself arrived in Vienna on 14 March, and Freud noted that on the very next day both his apartment and the offices of the *Verlag* were inspected by brown-shirted Nazis. Martin was held prisoner all day, but his captors failed to find any compromising documents in the offices; neither did they find anything useful for their purposes in Freud's apartment. Naturally enough there was international concern for Freud's welfare. Ernest Jones planned to utilise his connections with the British government and Marie Bonaparte intended to make full use of her royal connections. The issue reached the highest levels. Heinrich Himmler wanted all the analysts remaining in Vienna to be put into prison, but Hermann Göring restrained him. Meanwhile the American Secretary of State, Cordell Hull, informed President Roosevelt of Freud's plight, and Hull, on the President's instructions, told the American Ambassador in Germany, Hugh Robert Wilson, to pursue the matter with the German government. The aim was to try and arrange for Freud and his family to go to Paris. The Nazis were concerned, however, that Freud should not leave the country: they had confiscated his passport.

Jones flew to Vienna to try and expedite Freud's departure but found that a major obstacle was Freud's own reluctance to leave, due to his poor health and conviction that no country would welcome a feeble old man. He finally won him round but was then confronted with the question of the expense of the enterprise, as Freud wanted to take his entire family and that of his doctor with him, sixteen people in all. William Bullitt also did his best to negotiate financial help from the American government. Finally this issue was solved by the aid of Marie Bonaparte and Anna's close friend, Dorothy Burlingham. There still remained the problem, however, of obtaining permission from the Austrian authorities for Freud's departure, and, as Freud preferred to go to England, of securing residence permits for the whole family in that country. On 22 March there occurred an incident which put the success of the whole venture at risk: Anna Freud was arrested by the Gestapo.

Exactly what happened at Gestapo headquarters remains uncertain, but Anna was in severe danger of being taken off with other arrested Jews to a possible horrendous fate. She was interrogated about the nature of the International Psychoanalytic Society, and managed somehow to persuade her captors that it was a purely scientific organisation. Freud spent the entire day pacing up and down the apartment, endlessly smoking cigars. Finally, at seven o'clock in the evening, Anna was released. This event, above all others, undoubtedly persuaded Freud of the necessity of flight. But there were still bureaucratic hurdles to overcome. All kinds of conditions and financial payments had to be settled first. One of these was the so-called 'flight tax', the *Reichsfluchtssteuer*, imposed on all Jews who wished to leave the country. The assets of the Viennese Psychoanalytic Society were seized, including all the property of the *Verlag* and the library. The Nazis also tried to get their hands on Freud's works, but Martin, foreseeing the danger, had already posted them off to Switzerland. Marie Bonaparte made sure that all the financial demands of the Nazis were met, and she and Anna together sorted out all the bureaucratic and legal problems facing the family.

There was little that Freud himself could do in the circumstances, and he spent his time sorting out books, papers and his collection of antiquities. He even managed to spend a little time writing, on two utterly different projects: the book on *Moses and Monotheism* and, together with Anna, the translation of a short book that Marie Bonaparte had written in memory of her dog, Topsy. The settling of Freud's affairs dragged on, as he reported in a letter to his son Ernst in early May. Finally there was just one more formality to go through: the Gestapo demanded that Freud sign a document confirming that they had not treated him badly. Freud signed, but added at his own instigation a defiant comment, very risky in the circumstances, but with an irony that was presumably lost on the Nazis: 'I can heartily recommend the Gestapo to everyone' ('*Ich kann die Gestapo jedermann auf das beste empfehlen*').[16]

The Freuds did not leave Austria together. Minna Bernays had left on 5 May, accompanied by Dorothy Burlingham; Martin left on the 14th. His daughter Mathilde and her husband managed to get away on the 24th. Freud, Martha and Anna had to wait till 2 June before they finally received permission to travel. They departed on 4 June in the company of two faithful maids, one of whom, Paula Fichtl, was to remain indispensable to the family after Freud's death. It had been planned that his doctor, Max Schur, would accompany them but he himself was afflicted with appendicitis and could not travel. He was not able to join them in London until 15 June. Instead a friend of Anna's, Dr Josephine Stross, accompanied them to keep a check on Freud's health.

They travelled on the Orient Express via Paris, where they spent about twelve hours in the home of Marie Bonaparte, who was able to assure Freud that the gold he had wisely invested in as security in case of disaster had been safely transferred for him. They then travelled on the night ferry to Dover and thence to Victoria Station in London, where the train was diverted onto a platform away from the curious eyes of press and public. They were welcomed by station officials, Ernest Jones and his wife, and Martin and Mathilde. While Anna stayed behind with Ernst to deal with the luggage, Ernest Jones drove the immediate members of the family past famous sights of London to the house that Ernst had rented for them as a temporary residence at 39, Elsworthy Gardens. Here Freud was particularly delighted with the garden, which had a view towards Primrose Hill and Regent's Park.

It took some time before the family was properly settled. Minna had already arrived but was confined to bed on the first floor, and Sigmund, who could not climb stairs easily, was unable to see her. Eventually she was taken to a nursing home. Freud, who had long had a love of dogs, was also missing his chow, Lün, who had to undergo quarantine restrictions for six months. He was also concerned at having had to leave his four elderly sisters, Dolfi, Rosa, Paula and Marie, in Vienna. He had left them some money and later in the year Marie Bonaparte endeavoured unsuccessfully to help them to escape to France. Fortunately for Freud he never learned of their eventual fate: incineration in one of the Nazi death camps.

Before long Sigmund was settling down to work on the Moses book, and soon many distinguished guests were calling on him, including H.G. Wells again and the Zionist leader Chaim Weizmann. On 19 July Stefan Zweig came with the surrealist artist Salvador Dali, who made a strong positive impression on Freud. On 22 July Freud recorded that he had started work on yet another work, the *Outline of Psychoanalysis*, one of his most concise accounts, which was however to be left unfinished.

While the family's eventual permanent home was being prepared they had to move for a while to the Esplanade Hotel in Warrington Crescent. All this time Freud was suffering further complications of his cancerous condition, and he had to be transferred to a clinic, where Schur and other specialists decided that another operation would be necessary, summoning the surgeon Pichler from Vienna to perform the operation on 8 September. Eventually, on 16 September, Martha and Paula Fichtl moved into 20 Maresfield Gardens and Freud and Anna followed on the 27th. Although it had no special view, Freud was delighted with the garden, front and back, and, with the help of Paula, the antiquities and other belongings were soon arranged so that he could enjoy them.

Although he was becoming steadily weaker, Freud managed to continue writing and to treat three patients. And despite opposition from many sources, especially Jewish ones, Freud was determined to finish the Moses book and have it published. He was also negotiating with an English publisher to bring out a new German edition of his works.

Near the end of January 1939, Freud was visited by Leonard and Virginia Woolf, who were the owners of the Hogarth Press, publishers of the English editions of his works. Leonard Woolf was greatly impressed by Freud, likening him to an extinct volcano, but Virginia described him as a shrunken old man with eyes like a monkey.[17] In fact Freud's health was declining rapidly, and by February he was having to take painkillers regularly, something he had always disdained. During the coming months he was to become more and more dependent on the attentions of Anna and the personal care of Dr Schur. Schur had to be away in America for the celebration of Freud's eighty-third birthday in May, but Marie Bonaparte managed to be there, as did the French performer Yvette Guilbert. Then, on 19 May, Freud recorded a triumph of which he was especially proud: the appearance in English translation of *Moses and Monotheism*. The work aroused, as was to be expected, general outrage in the Christian press.

When Schur returned in July, he found Freud's condition greatly deteriorated. He was still conducting analyses and managing to write letters, but by 1 August he felt he could no longer cope with analysing patients. As his cancerous jaw became worse it emitted an unpleasant rotting smell and even Lün, his beloved chow, shrunk away from him. The pain was becoming more and more intense, yet still Sigmund was able to follow international events in the newspapers. When Germany marched into Poland on 1 September, Schur moved into the Freud house in case of an air raid. After Britain declared war on Germany on 3 September, Freud's bed was moved to the safest part of the house. The suffering was becoming unbearable but now Freud refused all sedation. It is known that the last book read by him was Balzac's *La Peau de Chagrin*. He told Schur that it was the right book for a man in his condition to read.

On 21 September Freud took Schur's hand and reminded him of the agreement they had made many years ago. Schur had not forgotten. Freud said that if Anna agreed they should end the torture. There was no sense in his life continuing. Schur injected Freud with three centigrams of morphine, one centigram more than the normal dose. Later Schur repeated the dose, and then administered a final one the next day. At three o'clock in the morning on 23 September 1939, after having been in a coma for some time, the founder of psychoanalysis died.

The Legacy

Freud's ideas quite simply revolutionised the way people of multifarious disciplines, philosophies, and belief systems conceived of the nature of the human mind. The ideas did not come out of the blue, having complex roots in cultural and scientific developments in Europe stretching back over many centuries. But Freud forced them to the forefront of our attention, demanded that full weight be given to the role of unconscious drives and especially to sexuality in the mental life of human beings. Whether his theoretical system, which he called psychoanalysis, is a true science, a mode of interpretation, or a personal mythology, the brainchild of one man, will continue to be debated by intellectuals, but what cannot be denied is the extensive influence of his ideas.

There are few areas of intellectual endeavour which have remained untouched by Freud's ideas: psychology and psychiatry, philosophy, sociology and anthropology, as well as religion, literature and art, to name but the most obvious areas. Psychoanalysis itself has continued to flourish long after its founder's death, though often in many different forms, with emphases and new formulations which Freud himself would never have condoned. Subsequent thinkers who have considered themselves to be psychoanalysts have indeed rarely adhered unquestioningly to Freud's original concepts, and to be a psychoanalyst nowadays implies entering into a constant critical dialogue with its exponents in the past. Indeed some of the most fruitful insights have come from critical responses to Freud's assumptions. In particular this is true of writers on child psychology and on the psychology of women's problems: Freud's ideas about women have provoked strong criticism amongst feminists. And within the psycho-analytic fold itself there has been an influential line of women analysts, from Anna Freud to Melanie Klein and Karen Horney. Critical responses have also led to considerable divergences from and complete reformulations of classic Freudian concepts, as in the work of Jacques Lacan, D.W. Winnicott and Heinz Kohut.

Even those who do not consider themselves to be intellectual are indebted to Freud in much of the very language they use. Who has not at some time noted their own or someone else's 'Freudian slip'? And this is true not only of speakers of English and German, but of speakers of many other languages too, which have their own translations of his concepts. 'Freudian' has long been an entry in all English language dictionaries, as have 'unconscious', 'subconscious', 'repression', 'neurosis' etc., which, though they may have been in use before Freud, now have indisputable Freudian connotations. There are also other specialist terms associated with his name: 'ego', 'super-ego','id' and 'libido'. And many concepts have acquired broader usage and implications through his reinterpretations, such as 'sexuality' and 'instincts'.

These are all parts of Freud's intellectual legacy, of his theory of the mind. His legacy as a man cannot be so easily defined. He is certainly remembered as being determined in the pursuit of truth, but also as being equally determined to defend the truths of his findings against any attempts to water them down. Not that he believed that it was ever possible to discover absolute truth about anything, as he once said to Stefan Zweig: 'There is as little chance of finding a hundred per cent truth as there is of finding a hundred per cent alcohol!'[18]

As the focus of this biography is on the man and not on the work, perhaps the final image of him should be that retained by

Stefan Zweig from one of his last meetings with Freud. He found that age, illness and the prospect of death had mellowed the man, and made him more human:

Age had only made him more gentle, and the trials he had overcome had made him more forbearing. Sometimes now he would make tender gestures, which I had previously never known this reserved man to make; he would put an arm around one's shoulder, and behind his glinting spectacles his eyes would be looking at you more warmly.[19]

Notes

1. Jones, vol I, 1953, p. 21.
2. Jones, vol I, 1953, pp. 36–9.
3. Freud, 'An Autobiographical Study', trans. James Strachey, London, Hogarth, 1935.
4. Jones, vol I, 1953, p. 224 et seq.
5. Freud, *Briefe an Wilhelm Fliess, 1887–1904*, 1986, letter of Dec 8., 1895.
6. Gay, 1988, pp. 138–9.
7. Jones, vol I, 1953, p. 341.
8. Jones, vol II, 1955, p. 139.
9. Jones, vol II, 1955, p. 179.
10. Letter to Sandor Ferenczi, Oct. 25, 1918.
11. Jones, vol II, 1955, p. 201.
12. Letter to Sandor Ferenczi, Jan. 2, 1927.
13. Gay, 1988, pp. 553–62.
14. Jones, vol III, 1957, p. 182.
15. Letter to Lou Andreas-Salomé, Jan. 6, 1935.
16. Martin Freud, *Freud*, p. 217.
17. Virginia Woolf, *The Diary of Virginia Woolf*, Vol V, *(1936–41)*, ed. Anne Olivier Bell, 1984, p. 202.
18. Stefan Zweig, *Die Welt von Gestern*, 1942 (2003), p. 474. Translated by the author.
19. ibid. p. 477. Translated by the author.

Select bibliography

A list of Freud's major works would be too long to include in the present book, and readers are recommended to consult the detailed bibliographies in the *Standard Edition* of his works and those in more extensive biographies. All of the works mentioned in the present book are also available in various paperback editions.

Collections of Freud's works

Gesammelte Werke, (in 18 volumes) Imago, London, 1940–1952, and Fischer, Frankfurt a.M., from 1960.

The Standard Edition of the Complete Psychological Works of Sigmund Freud, (in 24 volumes) The Hogarth Press, London, 1953–1974.

Note: Freud's letters are available in various editions, mostly identified by Freud's name and that of the recipient in each case.

Biographical Studies

Clark, Ronald W., *Freud: The Man and the Cause*, New York, 1980.

Freud, Martin, *Glory Reflected. Sigmund Freud – Man and Father,* Angus and Robertson, 1957.

Gay, Peter, *Freud, A Life for Our Time*, New York, 1988.

Jones, Ernest, *The Life and Work of Sigmund Freud*, New York, vol I (1953), vol II (1955), vol III (1957).

Schur, Max, *Freud, Living and Dying*, International Psychoanalysis Library, 1972.

Other Works Referred To

Woolf, Virginia, *The Diary of Virginia Woolf*, ed. Anne Olivier Bell, 1984.

Zweig, Stefan, *Die Welt von Gestern*, Fischer, 1942 (2003).

Biographical note

Dr David Carter has taught at St Andrews and Southampton universities in the UK and has been Professor of Communicative English at Yonsei University, Seoul. He has published on psychoanalysis, literature, drama, film history and applied linguistics, and now works freelance as a writer, journalist and translator. He has published books on the Belgian author Georges Simenon and Literary Theory, as well as in the field of film studies, the most recent being *East Asian Cinema and The Western*. For Hesperus he has translated Georges Simenon's *Three Crimes*, Honoré de Balzac's 'Sarrasine' and Klaus Mann's *Alexander*.

SELECTED TITLES FROM HESPERUS PRESS

Brief Lives

Author	Title
Anthony Briggs	*Brief Lives: Leo Tolstoy*
Andrew Brown	*Brief Lives: Gustave Flaubert*
Andrew Brown	*Brief Lives: Stendhal*
Richard Canning	*Brief Lives: E.M. Forster*
Richard Canning	*Brief Lives: Oscar Wilde*
David Carter	*Brief Lives: Honoré de Balzac*
Robert Chandler	*Brief Lives: Alexander Pushkin*
Melissa Valiska Gregory and Melisa Klimaszewski	*Brief Lives: Charles Dickens*
Gavin Griffiths	*Brief Lives: Joseph Conrad*
Patrick Miles	*Brief Lives: Anton Chekhov*
Andrew Piper	*Brief Lives: Johann Wolfgang von Goethe*
Alan Shelston	*Brief Lives: Elizabeth Gaskell*
Fiona Stafford	*Brief Lives: Jane Austen*

Classics and Modern Voices

Author	Title	Foreword writer
Honoré de Balzac	*Colonel Chabert*	A.N. Wilson
Honoré de Balzac	*Sarrasine*	Kate Pullinger
Honoré de Balzac	*The Vendetta*	
Marquis de Sade	*Virtue*	
Stendhal	*Memoirs of an Egotist*	Doris Lessing
Stendhal	*On love*	A.C. Grayling

HESPERUS PRESS

Hesperus Press is committed to bringing near what is far –
far both in space and time. Works written by the greatest
authors, and unjustly neglected or simply little known in
the English-speaking world, are made accessible through
new translations and a completely fresh editorial approach.
Through these classic works, the reader is introduced to
the greatest writers from all times and all cultures.

For more information on Hesperus Press, please visit our
website: **www.hesperuspress.com**